Praise for
Own Your Everyday

"Through engaging storytelling and heartfelt wisdom, Jordan invites us to step fully into the present moment. In a world where we often feel pressured to move forward as quickly as possible, the words that fill these pages shine light on this beautiful truth: there is a fulfilling life to be lived right here, where we are. This book is a conversation over coffee for the soul, and you will be sure to walk away encouraged to 'own your everyday.'"

—MORGAN HARPER NICHOLS, artist and poet

"Authentic, intuitive, and compassionate, Jordan clears the clutter from our minds and hearts while enthusiastically guiding us to discover our own authentic purpose. Along the way, we learn that our purpose is accessible because it's less about us and more about becoming a safe place for others, so we can leave a lasting impact on those around us."

—JESSICA HONEGGER, author, founder and co-CEO
of Noonday Collection

"There are those rare books you come across from time to time that make you feel like you are drinking from a fire hydrant. This is one of those books. Jordan brilliantly teaches, encourages, and convicts you all at the same time! Alyssa and I are so thankful for her willingness to lay it all out there in these pages and to lead us to a more firm and promising purpose!"

— JEFFERSON BETHKE, best-selling author of *Jesus > Religion* and *It's Not What You Think*

"Jordan offers a refreshing, relatable, and inspiring perspective on figuring out what God has purposed you to do and who He is purposing you to be. Each chapter is full of empowering stories and truths that will help you overcome whatever fears are holding you back and whatever lies are robbing you of joy, so that you can discover and fulfill your purpose. This book will meet you right where you are with a giant hug, while also give you a little kick in the pants."

—AUDREY ROLOFF, coauthor of *A Love Letter Life,* founder of Always More, cofounder of Beating50Percent

"Jordan is bursting with contagious joy, and this book is just an overflow. Prepare to be challenged and loved all at the same time."

— JENNIE ALLEN, author of *Nothing to Prove,* founder and visionary of IF:Gathering

"I love that Jordan addresses how the immense focus on finding our purpose often distracts us from enjoying the present and living out our purpose. As a struggling perfectionist myself, I related so much to the idea of the internal pressure we put on ourselves to perform and achieve. *Own Your Everyday* gave me the greatest encouragement to be myself."

—LAUREN SCRUGGS KENNEDY, influencer, author, entrepreneur

"Jordan truly has wisdom beyond her years, and this book is packed with both practical and beautiful ways to live out our God-given purpose! Right from the beginning, Jordan's heart bleeds through, and her honesty is so refreshing and relatable. This book will be such a gift to women!"

—CHRISTY NOCKELS, singer, songwriter, and creator of *The Glorious in the Mundane* podcast

"Jordan is wonderfully candid and vulnerable about how she found her ultimate redemptive purpose despite worldly obstacles of rejection, comparison, and expectation. She dives into our hearts by sharing both tear-jerking and laughable stories of her faith from childhood to current day. Each page is relatable and profound, yet beautifully simple."

—SARAH ROSE SUMMERS, Miss USA 2018

"I love how Jordan makes the topic of finding your purpose a sweet conversation as opposed to something ominous, impossible, and scary. Her whimsical stories remind you that we're all on the same journey—days filled with seemingly random moments that are really nudges from heaven. Each reminder about who you are, whose you are, and why you're really here is like an on-time hug mixed with a little kick in the pants too! If you're a fellow recovering perfectionist who tends to overcomplicate and overanalyze, *Own Your Everyday* invites you to pause. Jordan reminds us that even in the midst of mess and imperfection, we're already enough. This book is a call to stop striving and searching for answers externally and to start looking within. When we do, we're in for the adventure of a lifetime!"

—MARSHAWN EVANS DANIELS, reinvention strategist
for women, TV personality, and founder of
SheProfits.com

OWN YOUR EVERYDAY

JORDAN LEE DOOLEY

OWN YOUR EVERYDAY

OVERCOME THE PRESSURE TO PROVE AND SHOW UP FOR WHAT YOU WERE MADE TO DO

WATERBROOK

Own Your Everyday

All Scripture quotations, unless otherwise indicated, are taken from the Holy Bible, English Standard Version, ESV® Text Edition® (2016), copyright © 2001 by Crossway Bibles, a publishing ministry of Good News Publishers. All rights reserved. Scripture quotations marked (NIV) are taken from the Holy Bible, New International Version®, NIV®. Copyright © 1973, 1978, 1984, 2011 by Biblica Inc.® Used by permission. All rights reserved worldwide.

Hardcover ISBN 978-0-7352-9149-2
eBook ISBN 978-0-7352-9150-8

Published in the United States by WaterBrook, an imprint of the Crown Publishing Group, a division of Penguin Random House LLC, New York.

WATERBROOK® and its deer colophon are registered trademarks of Penguin Random House LLC.

Library of Congress Cataloging-in-Publication Data
Names: Dooley, Jordan Lee, author.
Title: Own your everyday: overcome the pressure to prove and show up for what you were made to do / Jordan Lee Dooley.
Description: First Edition. | Colorado Springs: WaterBrook, 2019.
Identifiers: LCCN 2018031822| ISBN 9780735291492 (hardcover) | ISBN 9780735291508 (electronic)
Subjects: LCSH: Christian women—Religious life.
Classification: LCC BV4527 .D66 2019 | DDC 248.8/43—dc23
LC record available at https://lccn.loc.gov/2018031822

Printed in the United States of America
2019

10

SPECIAL SALES
Most WaterBrook books are available at special quantity discounts when purchased in bulk by corporations, organizations, and special-interest groups. Custom imprinting or excerpting can also be done to fit special needs. For information, please email special marketscms@penguinrandomhouse.com or call 1-800-603-7051.

*For Nana. Thank you for teaching me
to never stop taking big steps.*

Contents

Your Brokenness Is Welcome Here

Hey, friend. My name is Jordan, and I'm a recovering perfectionist with a chronic need to achieve. I figure it's always best to start with honesty.

Now, I know you're probably trying to decide if this book is worth your time. So I'm going to tell you right out of the gate why I wrote it and why I believe it's important for you to read.

The number one question I get asked by blog readers, podcast listeners, social media followers, and even clients is something along the lines of "How do I find my purpose?" or "How do I figure out what I'm supposed to do with my life?" All of these women are different—some are making the transition into or out of college, navigating marriage or motherhood, or finding their place in the workforce. These women are taking steps to establish themselves in this big world but are feeling pressure to figure out exactly where they ought to land as soon as humanly possible.

Sometimes when I get these questions, I want to reach through the screen, hug a stranger's neck, and say, "Girl, chill. You don't have to have it all mapped out today, okay? And even if you did, you'd probably find that something would shake up those plans tomorrow anyway. Take a breath!"

Unfortunately, the reach-through-the-screen feature hasn't been created yet, so this book is my best attempt. We all want to make our mark, find meaning in the mayhem, and discover what makes our lives special, unique, and even notable. At least I do . . . and the girls who reach out to me with these questions do. I'd be willing to bet that you do too.

Now I want to take it a step further and ask you a question: Do you ever feel pressure to find your purpose—to find the reason you're on this earth and what it is that makes your life count?

Of course you do.

It seems everywhere I look, everybody is telling us to "go after our dreams" or "find our purpose." That's great and inspirational, but what about those of us who don't quite have our dreams, aspirations, and plans perfectly figured out? You know what I'm talking about, don't you?

In today's culture there is so much pressure to figure out

our future or get started on our dream. Even stepping into a Sunday sermon, you'll hear about how you need to find your calling. Yet those of us who haven't quite nailed these things begin to feel like a failure. It seems we should have figured this out by the time we finished school, if not before.

I've honestly found this pressure and entire perspective on purpose to be a bit dangerous because it implies that our purpose is something we have to search for, find, and grab hold of, whether it's a job, a title, a degree, or business. I'm afraid we've shrunk purpose down to what we do on the outside rather than who we are on the inside. Does it include what we do? Definitely. However, I often wonder whether we've boiled it down to *just* that and, as a result, get stuck in our own heads when we don't know what to do next. I mean, what about those of us with multiple passions, various ideas, or unfigured-out dreams?

Quite honestly, half my dreams change from Sunday to Tuesday in a given week. Sure, I have some big ideas, but sometimes it's difficult to determine if they're just ideas I *could* do or things I actually *should* do. Perhaps you relate to this feeling. Or maybe the things you've been chasing are other people's dreams for you—or expectations of you—and the weight of that is heavy. Perhaps the reason you've been feeling a little stuck is because you've put too much pressure on yourself to figure it all out.

You know that feeling that comes when you scroll Instagram and it seems everyone else has her life figured out? Or how you start to sweat as graduation or marriage or another big milestone approaches and you think, *I have GOT to figure out my life?* Or the way your stomach drops when your dad calls during those awkward postgrad years and asks about your plans for the future? Or when your pastor talks about callings and you just sit there and wish you could call God and say, *Hey, so, do You think You can just get to the point and tell me what to do with my life? All this waiting around feels pretty ineffective.*

Yeah, those are the feelings I'm tackling in this book because I know the search can seem endless and the pressure is real.

While I don't know what you're facing today, I do know that the pressure to prove ourselves can cause us to expend a lot of time and energy looking for but perhaps not actually fulfilling our purpose.

In fact, when I began to examine the pressure I felt to find my purpose, I discovered something: Maybe my purpose isn't actually something I need to *find.* Maybe I've been sitting on it all along but I've been so distracted by the pressure to prove that I've been looking at it all wrong.

When we're always under pressure to find something that *isn't actually lost*—believing we must find it outside ourselves—or when we're distracted with running around trying to prove we are enough, we cannot accomplish what we're meant to do. Know why? Because *the pressure to prove* and *true purpose* cannot coexist.

As I looked more closely at my own life, I found a toxic trio made up of insecurities, expectations, and the pressure to prove. When I gave too much power to the toxic trio, I allowed these three things to create mental roadblocks or barriers that held me back and got me off track from what really matters. Some of these mind-sets I get stuck in include impostor syndrome, disappointment, shame, comparison, perfectionism, and distraction. When I operate from these places, I don't love like I should. I don't notice the divine moments God invites me into. I don't work well but rather just work hard. The list goes on.

I hold myself back. I'm the culprit here. Yes, I—not someone else's expectations of me and not a lack of knowledge, resources, or qualifications—hold myself back from living a purposeful life. In other words, it's usually my mind-set, not my skill set, that holds me back.

However, when I relentlessly fight to realign with my true purpose, prepare for the challenges of life, and equip myself with the perspective it takes to break through the pressure (rather than simply avoiding or ignoring it), everything changes.

I still don't have it all figured out, but I have discovered some practical steps to overcome these barriers and live my purpose right where I'm at. And I want to pass them on to you.

I believe it's important to discuss this for a number of reasons. Namely, we often view barriers such as comparison and perfectionism as things that hold us back from purpose, but I'm here to argue that *purpose is the very way out of the traps we get stuck in.*

So here's my plan: In these pages I'll share simple steps to overcome the pressure to prove by channeling the purpose *we already have right where we are,* regardless of our circumstances, struggles, and shortcomings. By the time you finish this book, you will have had some eye-opening moments as you identify blind spots and unproductive habits you may not even realize you've been living with. You will have practical tools to take with you—tools that will help you move from living under the pressure to prove to living out a life of purpose.

My goal is that this resource will not only give you a swift kick in the pants but also feel like a warm hug or chat with your best friend (and that you'll want to share it with all your gals too).

Together we're going to get unstuck. We're going to stop blaming everyone and everything else for what hasn't gone right and start taking responsibility for our lives right where we are (without the pressure to control or figure everything out). And above all else, we're going to take practical steps to break through the pressure and walk in line with this purpose we're looking for. I don't care where you come from, what you believe, or how frustrated you might be. You are welcome here, just as you are. You don't have to be fancy. You don't have to have an impressive résumé, income level, or any other kind of status symbol. You just need to take small steps with me.

Are you ready to do what it takes to live an intentional life? To push past insecurities, expectations, and the pressure to prove so you can simply start showing up for what you were made to do? Let's do this.

Part 1

Where Do I Start?

1

You Can't Walk Through Walls

Here are a few things you should know about me: I don't have a master's degree in anything. I haven't saved someone from a burning building recently (or ever). I had a chicken named Pickle (I say *had* because she was recently escorted to chicken heaven, thanks to the not-so-friendly neighborhood owl). My favorite talent is that I can clap with one hand (which makes me look a little ridiculous flapping my hand around). Quite honestly, I'm a pretty average human being.

I just want to make sure we're on the same page, because there have been far too many times I've opened a book thinking the author puts her pants on differently than I do—as if she's a fancy-pants lady instead of an ordinary, imperfect human like me. Why do we do that? Why do we see people's names on book covers or their faces on TV or become followers of their social media and then get some weird idea in our heads that they're better than we are?

I've done it, and I'm sure you have too. So let me just set your expectations here. I'm not trying to be your pastor or your professor or your counselor. I'm your pal. We put our pants on the same way. And I hope you feel as though you're sitting on the floor eating pizza with me in our pajamas and not as though I'm talking at you from a pulpit.

Just to paint the scene, I'm currently sitting at my kitchen table wearing mismatched socks and an oversize T-shirt, and I could really use a shower. (Sometimes when you get on a writing roll, you just accept the troll look for the day and go into your cave.) It's not exactly glamorous over here.

That's my whole point, though. Who says we have to be glamorous to show up and do what we're made to do? Who says we've got to have a cool story to step into something bigger than ourselves? That narrative stops right here. Maybe if we quit assuming our talents are lame or our stories are boring or we have to be impressive to be impactful and instead just look a little deeper, we'll find something more powerful than what meets the eye.

That said, even if you are cooler than I am and you *have* saved somebody from a burning building or won a Nobel

Peace Prize, I still think we'll be friends. I believe we can have different experiences and still ultimately struggle with the same core issues: insecurities, unmet expectations, and the pressure to prove ourselves. I've been so wrapped up in labels and perceived expectations that I nearly lost myself. If any of this resonates with you, get comfortable and let's have a nice long chat.

Now that we've found some common ground in our mutual humanness, I want to start at the beginning of my story, with some of my earliest and most treasured memories.

Big Step

One particular memory is so vivid that I can almost smell the corn tortillas searing on the stove and hear Nana's thick Hispanic accent. Though decades have passed, I still remember the games I'd play with my grandma in her tiny one-bedroom apartment. I loved those times when it was just the two of us, when she'd make my favorite food and we'd giggle and play games until all hours of the night. (Bedtime never existed during sleepovers at Nana's house.)

As I played with my dolls on the floor one evening, Nana reached for a roll of masking tape, ripped off a long piece, and stuck it to the fuzzy brown carpet next to me. She placed another and another, until several long pieces formed a lopsided square around my six-year-old self. Then she tossed the remainder of the roll to the side.

"Ta-da!" she said. *"Es una casa, mi Jordan preciosa!"* ("It's a house, my precious Jordan!") A gap, an empty space on one side, marked the doorway to get in and out of our imaginary house. Stepping over the cockeyed lines of tape that marked pretend walls wouldn't do. Why? Because you can't walk through walls.

I'm always amazed when I realize these simple, seemingly insignificant childhood games we played had powerful lessons tucked inside. Doors are essential in life. Doors are the only way we allow others in and the only way we step out. They're also the only way we move beyond the little walls we tend to build around ourselves in an effort to avoid vulnerability or possible betrayal. Perhaps in our most simple and unobserved experiences, such as mine with Nana, we learn more about the purpose tucked deep inside us than in the milestones and moments we publicize on social media.

This was just one of many make-believe games Nana and I played together. In our enchanted world, such as that imaginary house made of tape, I had a sanctuary in which to dream. I had a safe place to be anything I could imagine, and I loved it.

This is also where my childhood nickname, Sparkles, originated. I admit that's a horrendously embarrassing nickname. But it was oddly accurate. I wanted to sparkle, to shine, to be beautiful, and to be seen. Don't we all?

Nana and I often switched roles when we played make-believe. Sometimes she pretended to be the child so I could be the grandma. Other times she was the customer so I could be the chef. This time, though, she was the patient and I was the nurse.

"Knock, knock," she said. I reached out my arm and acted as if I were opening a door, welcoming her into my clinic. She extended her leg dramatically as she moved through the doorway—the gap in the tape. I knew what was coming.

"Big step!" we said together.

"Big step" was our thing, our own little tradition. Nana encouraged me when I was a toddler simply by coming alongside me, taking my hand, and showing me how to take a big step. The big step became part of nearly every game we played together. We didn't do anything without taking big, fearless steps. Together we'd each peel our toes off the floor, simultaneously stretch out our right legs, and say, "Big step!"

As our toes hit a new place on the floor ahead of us, we celebrated, often dancing to a silly tune Nana made up on the spot. Other times we'd give each other a high five, and sometimes, when Mom wasn't looking, Nana would sneak me some of my favorite candy, gummy bears, as if to say, *Well done, little one.*

Big step.

Even into my adolescent years, sweet Nana whispered that phrase whenever I felt afraid, unsure, or insecure. When I was nervous about playing the part of an Oompa Loompa in the middle school play *Charlie and the Chocolate Factory,* she slipped her weathered hand into mine, which had been painted orange, and gave me a wink as if to remind me: big step.

Before I ever really understood the depth of what she was teaching me, Nana dared me to dream, to be bold in pursuing the path God lays right before me, and to take fearless steps with purpose *before* I figured anything else out.

One big step. That's all it took to give me the courage and boldness to step out a little farther and walk a little taller as a young girl. I still believe that's all it takes for you and me—one big step. At first glance this idea might seem cliché—silly, even. But I think we often forget that every big step in life is really just a series of tiny movements and small decisions that add up, becoming the very thing that allows us to move from living in insecurity to living out our destiny.

One Last Big Step

Several years later, Nana got really sick. She'd been ill for a while when I found her one Tuesday afternoon banging her hands violently on a wall, lost and confused and trying to escape her nursing home—the place that kept her safe. Turns out you really can't walk through walls, even if you want to. I wrapped my arms around her to calm her, but she didn't recognize me. A nurse came to the rescue. I gulped, and with a lump in my throat, I fought back tears. Nana had always been a safe place for me when I felt afraid as a little girl. But now, when I tried to be a safe place for her, when I tried to wrap her in a protective embrace and be her refuge when she felt afraid, she didn't know me.

As Nana would say, *Oh my stars.*

We finally calmed Nana and got her seated. Alzheimer's was winning the battle for her mind, and somehow it was managing to break my spirit too. Then the nurse handed me a plastic cup of peaches and asked whether I'd like to help feed my grandmother.

Seriously? No, I don't want to feed her. She's supposed to feed me! I wanted to respond.

But I didn't say anything. I kindly accepted the plastic cup of preserved fruit and asked Nana to open her mouth, just as she had asked me to do many years before. My mind was swirling. *Is this real life? What is happening?* What do you do when one of your very best friends, one of your childhood heroes, the one who pretended to be sick and broken so you could pretend to nurse her back to health, becomes truly sick and broken? How do you handle it when the roles you played in that imaginary house of tape become reality? How do you cope with the disappointment when you hope she'll recognize your face but she doesn't?

I didn't know. My seventeen-year-old heart didn't have a clue. I searched every square inch of myself and came up without an answer worth more than that old roll of tape. Maybe you know how it is with brokenness like this. The kind we can't seem to control—the downward spiral of shame, sickness, or pain.

We stare into cups of peaches, searching for answers, hoping for a break from the breaking, wishing that somehow the damage will be reversed, and wondering where on God's green earth that light at the end of the tunnel is.

About a year later, I had just settled in for my first year at Indiana University when Mom called to tell me Nana had taken a turn for the worse. She didn't have much time left, and it was time to say goodbye.

Goodbye—a send-off, a word used when parting ways. How is it that the word we use when ending a phone call is the same one we whisper when we're about to be separated from someone who's slipping into eternity—a separation marked by the reality that we won't be able to just call each other back? When we're about to be divided by walls we can't leave a gap in, as we could with tape on the floor? Nana was about to take a big step into eternity, but this time I couldn't hold her hand the whole way.

I packed a bag, locked my college dorm room, hopped into the car Nana had passed down to me, and cried mascara-filled tears onto the steering wheel as I raced home. Somehow I managed to drive despite my blurred vision.

When I arrived at the nursing home, I found my mom sitting by Nana's side. I plopped down next to her and leaned over to kiss the pale skin on Nana's forehead, knowing this would be the last time. Within a few hours Nana took that big step into eternity, leaving the rest of us behind. The heart that had given so much light and love to my own young heart had no beats left. Mom's eyes filled with tears as I hugged her tight.

She squeezed back as if to wring the sadness out of both of us. Bearing burdens is just like that—leaning in, letting someone else's pain seep from her heart into ours. It means becoming a shelter for someone, often when our own heart is barely beating. But there's comfort in that. A purpose in it.

Purpose. There's profound purpose in simply meeting other people right where they are, in stepping into, not away from, their struggles and sharing them. Sometimes we can be so quick to offer consoling words and dry someone else's tears, when really the best thing we can do is let the tears flow and even absorb them. Bearing burdens doesn't mean fixing them. It means not allowing the other person to bear the load alone.

We sat there, Mom and I, waterworks and all. I wanted nothing more than to find a roll of masking tape and wrap it around my heart to keep it from falling apart. And maybe that's what I began to do. Maybe that's what we all do sometimes.

The Walls Were Only Make-Believe

When all the visiting, sharing, laughter, and tears surrounding Nana's funeral ended, I traveled back to campus and attempted to make the transition to college life and learn all that comes with adulting for the first time. That's a challenge in and of itself.

In the middle of an awkward transitional season, losing Nana added a curveball I wasn't prepared for. So I spent the subsequent months trying to wrap my life in the things I thought would hold me together, in what I thought would keep me strong and secure when I felt as though I were falling apart. Academic accomplishments. A boyfriend. Leadership positions and résumé boosters. The whole nine yards.

It was like a strategy to distract myself from mourning. I thought if I filled my life with enough good things, covering up the internal feelings of insecurity with external Band-Aids, perhaps the sadness would somehow go away. I reasoned that the image I built up on the outside would somehow make me all better inside.

Over time I became the girl who kept up with the crowd on Friday night and still aced a test at eight o'clock on Monday morning, all while juggling eight billion extracurricular activities, clocking in at a part-time job, and training for a half marathon. I mean, why not?

You know, I used to hear the word *labels* and immediately think of negative things. Except when I look back at that season, it's obvious that reputation management and image maintenance are nothing more than sticking a bunch of labels and titles on ourselves that we assume others will perceive as positive. Seemingly good labels such as "the smart girl" or "the put-together girl" or "the grad student" can give a sense of confidence because of how others perceive us. However, they also create pressure to live up to the perceived expectations that come with those labels. If you're "the smart girl," you'd better not get a B on that test. If you're "the fit girl," you'd better not eat that cake. Whatever the word or label is, trying to live up to what we believe that ought to look like creates a lot of pressure. Of course, I didn't know that at that time. I thought looking strong meant being strong (spoiler alert: that's not always true).

Those labels I lived behind were like those lines of tape I played inside as a little girl. Behind them I could hide from the world and keep my insecurities a secret.

But those tape walls had never really kept me safe. They were just tape. They were only make-believe, after all. And perhaps the same is true for labels we live behind and boxes we get stuck inside. Maybe they're just made up in our own minds.

2

What Are You *Really* After?

Fun fact: when I feel insecure or off-balance, I look for acceptance. It's true. I remember the fall semester of my sophomore year of college, nearly an entire year after Nana passed away. I was beginning to want a place to belong, kind of like the one Nana had provided for me in my little tape houses as a girl, and I decided to do something I never thought I would: join a sorority.

When I signed up for recruitment, I wasn't sure what to expect, but more than anything, I hoped to fit in. I wanted to find a sorority house where I could cuddle up safely inside, basking in the sense of belonging I assumed it would bring.

On the first day, my Rho Gamma, or recruitment leader, handed me a schedule that told me where to be and when. Along with thousands of other hopeful girls, all of us in an unspoken competition for a limited number of spots, I was required to go to every single sorority house on campus. I was encouraged to put on my best smile and reminded not to talk about serious topics like religion or politics.

When I arrived at the first house, I slipped into a line of girls waiting for the sorority sisters inside to open the door. Dozens of beautiful young women stood in front of me, and another dozen lined up behind me.

It was a snowy January day, and everyone but me seemed to have received the memo about wearing the long sleek black jacket in style that year. I, on the other hand, wore a puffy pink jacket better suited to a ten-year-old in snow pants carrying a cool new sled than to a college gal with curled hair and high heels trying to appear sophisticated.

Have you ever been in one of those situations where you get ready for a dinner party or event thinking you totally look the part, only to show up and see everyone else got the memo for formal attire? And then you think, *Well, now I just feel like a sack of potatoes. Great* . . . Yeah, story of my life.

I looked down at my obnoxiously pink coat, and my mind began to race.

These girls are all wearing outfits way nicer than mine. Do they have better personalities too?

I look ridiculous. Why did I walk out of the house in this?

I probably won't even get in. What am I doing here?

Before I had a chance to answer any of those questions, the big front door swung open and dozens of girls inside jumped up and down perfectly in unison as they sang a song about how great their chapter was. As the song concluded, the sea of sorority sisters neatly split, and our line of potential new members, referred to as PNMs—at first I thought they called us PMS—filed inside.

Two beautiful girls invited me to sit down on one of the plush sofas in the formal living room, which featured marble columns and built-in bookshelves. This place was fancy with a capital *F*.

One twirled her hair as she asked question after question, while the other intently listened, interjecting only now and then. Wanting nothing more than to be wanted, I felt the pressure to prove I was likable and could fit right into their chapter. I rattled off everything I was involved in on campus, my academic achievements, and my philanthropic goals.

Between you and me, I had very little understanding of what *philanthropic* meant at the time, but I think I played it pretty cool, because they didn't seem to notice.

I am kind of an awkward person, though, so as I attempted to come off as cool and put together, I caught myself wondering whether they would notice the awkwardness hidden behind my lipstick grin.

Then a bell rang, and we PNMs filed out of the house and

shakily sprinted in heels to another house across campus to get in line and be interviewed all over again. Picture Bambi slipping around on the ice (with the addition of lipstick and a puffy pink coat). That was me.

On top of that, we had only about twenty minutes between one round and the next, so at any given time, I and thousands of other girls were wobble-sprinting around campus trying to make it to the next house, hop in line, and step through the door on time—each of us wanting to be wanted.

Maybe you've never gone through sorority recruitment, but you've felt that same pressure to prove yourself. You've felt that deep ache to be chosen, valued, and wanted. It may have been during a job interview or performance review. Or maybe you were hoping that the hunky guy in class would notice you or that your family would appreciate what you do.

Sis, nobody has it all figured out. We've all been awkward Bambis running around, hoping a little lipstick transforms us into Beyoncé. We've all wobbled around at one point or another, just needing to be wanted . . . or wanting to be needed.

I think we all want to be needed, believing our contribution counts. But more than that, we need to be wanted—treasured for who we are, not just used for what we bring to the table. Being wanted gives us more than a sense of purpose; it gives us the meaning, connection, and significance we crave—the very things that drive our ability to walk tall in our God-given purpose instead of wobbling around just trying to prove ourselves.

When I get caught up in the awkward wobble races, I end up falling further behind because I focus on portraying an image that doesn't actually exist instead of kicking off the heels and taking steps in the direction of what truly matters.

The truth? We'll miss who we're *made to be* when we focus on what we think we're *supposed to be*.

When we operate out of the pressure to prove ourselves instead of walking in line with the purpose already inside us right where we are, we'll always feel the need to keep up with and outrun others, to do something that's impressive and be somebody, in order to find our place and keep it. But what if life isn't about finding a safe place, holding our spot, or finishing first? What if it's about *becoming* a safe place? About being someone who makes others feel wanted? What if it's about taking a stand and stepping out with courage, even if that means we finish *last*?

Raise Your Hand If You Overthink Everything Too

Did your hand go up? Do you overthink half the opportunities you get? If so, you're in good company here. At the end of sorority recruitment, I received a bid—an invitation to join AOII. I felt a bit of relief to get one of these coveted spots, but that relief was coupled with a wave of insecurity. I tend to be an over-thinker, so I began questioning whether I should go through with it. I'm not kidding when I say that I almost didn't accept the invitation I thought I would have been thrilled to get.

I mean, I was terrified. I wondered what would happen if the sorority members were finally able to see the imperfections hidden behind the labels I'd wrapped my life in. *What if I don't make any friends? What if I don't fit in? Wait a second, didn't they say they have communal bathrooms? Maybe I should re-think this.*

But then someone told me there'd be free pizza at the welcome party. What college student turns down free pizza? As I began to make my way to the big house with the white columns, double doors, and wraparound staircase, I kept thinking, *What am I doing? This isn't me. I'm totally not cut out for this.*

When I stepped through the front door, however, my fears melted as dozens of enthusiastic girls welcomed me. I was handed a name tag, a tiara, and a pink feather boa. (Don't ask—it's a sorority thing.) Nervous as I was, I began to feel excited, too.

This was what I wanted! I thought I had found a safe place that would provide the acceptance and belonging I'd been looking for. That's all I wanted out of the deal—to make it in so I'd have a place to fit in and a clique to run with. I wanted a place at the table and a seat in the circle. I didn't see it then, but I see it now: sometimes my deepest desires reveal my deepest insecurities.

My biggest insecurity at the time was the fear of not being accepted. As I smiled for photos in my tiara and sparkly feather boa, I saw only the small, momentary purpose an organization like a sorority could serve for me—giving me a place to fit in and even a sense of worth and identity. My need to wedge myself into a group and the thought that it would somehow make me more confident reveal that I subconsciously believed I was not complete or confident unless I fit in a certain social circle.

However, I soon discovered God always has a bigger purpose for us than we have for ourselves. Looking back, I realize that season had little to do with fitting in and everything to do with finding out more about what I'm made for.

We can be so small minded sometimes, focusing only on making it through the door in front of us instead of opening the door of our hearts to see what God has for us. In doing so, we create limitations for ourselves, drawing lines based only on what we have the ability to see.

I love how Proverbs 16:9 says "the heart of man plans his way, but the LORD establishes his steps." This has become a verse I cling to when I look at where I am and don't quite understand what I'm doing here or there, or when I catch myself feeling so wrapped up in my expectations and insecurities that I risk overlooking the bigger plan at work.

An Unexpected Discovery

During my time in that big house, sharing a small space inside four cinder-block walls with three other girls, I began to look forward to the late-night laughter that turned into deep conversations about the meaning of life. I loved the spontaneous walks around campus that I'd take with a sister and the way we'd drop what we were doing to share a pint of ice cream when a friend went through a breakup. In those ordinary yet divine day-to-day moments, I got a peek at the purpose for which I'd been placed in that exact location.

In the residence where I thought I would merely find a place to fit in, I learned that I am made for friendship. And friendship is more than just fitting in.

As I swapped stories and traded advice with the friends I made there, it was as if my own interior walls began to crumble. A passion for the power of sisterhood—for coming alongside and empowering women—was sparked. And there was no stopping it. Fast-forward several years, and that passion has only grown. Hence, this book for you, sister friend.

Why do I tell you? Why should you care? Because through this experience I realized that God doesn't always have to work through big things to show us why we're here. He will use seemingly insignificant places to show us what we're really made for—even when we begin with selfish motives. In other words, the steps may seem small, but a bigger purpose is always at work.

We live in a world that says when we finally get that job, obtain that degree, or grab hold of that trophy or that title, we'll find our purpose. Over the years, though, that special space of sisterhood—those semesters I slept on an old bunk bed and stood in long lines for meals—taught me that purpose has little to do with the job or role I have, the season I'm in, or the setting I occupy. Rather, it has everything to do with the significance or meaning that drives my life and what I bring to those specific situations. If I tried to find my purpose in roles, seasons, or spaces, I'd always be chasing my purpose, never quite able to catch it. Those specifics could end or change, and my purpose would go right along with them.

I thought I needed to prove myself to find my place. I soon came to find out that life is so much better (with far less pressure) when we stop trying to fit in or find our place and instead step out, welcome others, and give them a place at the table— even if they're 1,000 percent different from us.

In fact, that's what inspired the creation of my shop tagline, "Your Brokenness Is Welcome Here." Living in a house with hundreds of sisters, I saw how women who support one another without judgment and comparison can be one of the most powerful forces on the planet. And I also know that when drama or judgment occurs, it can be one of the most damaging.

My friends in AOII taught me how to be a sister, a supporter, and a cheerleader. I learned what it means to love and welcome people who are both like me and different from me. That purpose doesn't change with specific roles and has extended far beyond my years in a sorority—into all of life.

So what's my point? If you're trying something new or stepping into a place or position you don't feel cut out for, you need to move forward anyway and drop your expectations at the door. You might be surprised by what you find and who you become one tiny decision at a time.

Small steps (before it all makes sense) really are the big steps.

3

Breakthrough Begins with You

Confession: I've tried so hard to pick at and pop a break-out that I've bruised my own face . . . on multiple occasions. Swelling happened. Ice packs have been involved. I have the scars to prove it. I'm sorry if that's TMI, but I'm telling you straight up because I need to get your attention.

Please, for the love of Pete, do not read this chapter lightly. I'm warning you: it'll probably hit your soul in the softest places, but it needs to be said because I think we waste a lot of time building an image we want the world to see instead of taking responsibility for breaking through the limits we create in our own heads and becoming who we're made to be.

I don't know what insecurities you struggle with on a daily basis, but one of mine has been acne.

I remember back in seventh grade, I attended a school where kids had to wear uniforms and girls weren't allowed to wear any kind of makeup to class. That was fine and dandy at first, but what's a thirteen-year-old girl to do when the boy she crushes on sits on her right in third period and she's got a massive zit on the right side of her face?

She finds a way to cover it up. Or, at least, I did. I tried my best to wear the makeup I had in a way that looked as natural and unnoticeable as possible. However, this was before the days when teenage girls could access dozens of video tutorials online to help with such a thing, so I winged it.

It worked at first; for a few days, I got away with it. But I had a teacher who could see makeup from a mile away. On day three of wearing makeup to school, in the middle of an ordinary afternoon, she noticed. I was called out in class and sent to the restroom to wash it off. When I returned, I felt raw and exposed, as though my big red pimple was practically waving at the class. Needless to say, things didn't work out with my crush. After I got busted and had to stop covering up my breakout, it cleared up fast. It was completely healed within a couple of days. Imagine that!

More recently, the last few years of my life have been a battle with cystic acne. If you're unfamiliar with what that is, it basically feels like your face is attacking itself. In other words, the breakouts aren't mere pimples. They are deep flare-ups, usually well beneath the surface and nearly impossible to pop, but the pressure is so bad that all you want to do is squeeze the snot out of them! If you try to break them too early, all you'll do is bruise your face or possibly make your skin bleed and swell more. I apologize for being graphic, but this is important, okay?

The pressure swelling beneath the surface hurts like heck, and when you look in the mirror, you feel like a total train wreck. It's a really unpleasant experience. For whatever reason, though, I just lived with it and accepted it as my reality for way too long.

By that, I mean it had been going on for over a year and a half when I finally realized I needed to take action to get it under control. I know, I know. You're sitting there thinking, *J, why didn't you just go to the doctor?*

You want to know the honest answer? I think I was slightly embarrassed by the fact that I was a married woman, an adult, dealing with deep, massive breakouts like that. Like, *Hello, puberty round two.* Yeah, no thanks. I'll pass.

So I lived in denial for a while because I'm one of those stubborn people who tend to take the approach of "Unless I'm dying, I'm not going to the doctor." (I know, that is dumb. I'm working on it.) Maybe I hate having my problems or insecurities diagnosed, because then I have to do the work it takes to actually deal with them.

After a while, though, I couldn't handle it anymore. My

face was so scarred, red, and bumpy that no amount of makeup coverage was cutting it anymore. I'm serious. My face was no longer a canvas. It was a battlefield crying for help.

When I finally did go to the dermatologist, barefaced with every dark scar, crusty scab, and lumpy red bump exposed, I wasn't sure what to expect. I just hoped he could fix me. This problem was not only embarrassing but also incredibly inconvenient because my job requires me to be in front of a camera somewhat regularly . . . and it was not getting any better.

I sat down on that weird crunchy paper on the exam table and tried not to shift my weight so it wouldn't crinkle under my butt. I already felt like a crusty barnacle. The last thing I needed was to be a crunchy one too. The doctor walked in and started the exam in the worst possible way for a girl who was already insecure about her face.

He shined a bright light on me and *took close-up pictures of my skin.* I immediately regretted the decision to come and wanted to crawl in a hole.

Yes, I realize this may be kind of dramatic. I'm aware the photos were for medical purposes. However, when you can hardly stand to go out into the world with your bare face exposed, the thought of someone—doctor or not—having an unedited photo of it on a device seems like the worst thing in the world. I tried to play it cool, pretending the photo evidence of my exposed insecurities did not bother me, when it totally did. I sat still as the doctor asked me what had been going on and what I'd been noticing with these flare-ups.

I told him that as soon as one would heal, another two would begin to form. Every time I took one step forward, I took two steps backward. He said, "Okay, so these breakouts are deep. They aren't just little clogged pores. They are being caused by something systemic."

I asked him to elaborate. He explained, "In other words, this isn't so much an issue of what's going on externally, on the surface, but internally, beneath the surface. It could be hormonal or bacterial and quite possibly is linked to diet or stress."

Next he asked about my skin-care routine. At first I told him all about how diligently I washed and moisturized my face every day, as if that would impress him. Then he asked about my makeup. I admitted I'd been wearing more makeup than I ever had before in an effort to cover up the dark scars and make the deep breakouts appear less obvious.

He stressed that while the root of these issues may not be the makeup, caking it on to cover up the wounds certainly wasn't helping my cause. I knew that, but I felt as though I didn't have a choice. Have you ever felt that way? Have you felt as if you had to cover up your flaws to feel adequate, even though doing so only made those perceived inadequacies worse? As if leaving them uncovered would be more damaging to your confidence than the long-term damage covering them actually caused?

It may seem superficial, but I'm telling you, sister: this is more than skin deep. One time my husband shared his theory about the whole cosmetics industry: "These makeup companies have got all you girls fooled," he said with a chuckle. "They sell you makeup, which is essentially expensive dirt that you put on your face but is supposed to make you feel more beautiful. Of course, it doesn't help the irritation and breakouts on your skin, so then they sell you products to undo the damage their dirt made worse. And they somehow convince you to buy more of their bottled dirt to cover up the breakouts the makeup irritated in the first place! It's this endless cycle you put your skin through, and they're rolling in the dough. If you didn't put the dirt on your skin to begin with, you'd probably have far less problems and fewer products piled up in your bathroom cabinets."

The first time he put it to me this way, I laughed out loud. But I also had to give him some credit. He wasn't totally wrong. Although I'm not arguing against makeup (and I'm sure every makeup sales rep is cringing and considering sending me an email saying, "Doesn't he know there are clean and healthy makeup products?"), let's just think about what he's saying here on a deeper level.

The man *was* onto something. And the whole debacle I was facing with my skin began to make a lot more sense. Covering up the surface only causes more problems beneath the surface, allowing the pesky insecurities to linger longer and have way more power over our lives than they deserve.

This principle doesn't apply only to skin care. I think we've become so used to covering up problems from the outside, focusing on our image and how others perceive us, that we forget to go deeper and deal with what's going on inside—what's actually causing the breakouts, flare-ups, and swells of insecurities.

When we get infected with expectations or when the pressure to prove swells, insecurity breaks out.

As my doctor said, the inflammation wasn't caused by something on the surface but rather by *something inside me.* Do you know what that means for you and me in a bigger way? It means we need to start looking at what's going on deeper, often in our hearts, instead of picking ourselves apart.

Start in the Heart

I'm going to switch gears here for a second, but I promise there's a reason. As a young girl, I became familiar with construction because while other ten-year-old girls played with Barbies and Polly Pockets, I learned about blueprints in the back of my dad's truck.

Dad owned a construction company, and the hard hats, toolboxes, and new building plans always intrigued me. Every now and then, I'd get to hear about the latest project as we rocked out to Elvis's greatest hits on the way to school. Dad would tell me about how one team had just broken ground while another team was wrapping up.

Regardless of what each project would become in the end, every single building started the same way: digging beneath the surface, creating a gaping hole in the ground, and removing dirt to make room for the foundation.

Those dad-and-daughter car rides taught me an invaluable lesson early in life: if you're going to build a solid foundation, breaking ground is nonnegotiable. Breaking through the hard layer on top, digging a hole in the earth, and removing the dirt that's settled there make room for something new and better.

Do you know what that means for you and me? It means we've got to break ground, or go beneath the surface, if we're ever going to break through insecurities, expectations, and the pressure to prove.

I don't know about you, but I'm stubborn and would rather skip that part. Some days I'd rather throw a concrete slab over the surface and build my life on that. My dad would tell you that might work for a little shed but not for a residential building. He'd explain how the ground moves when it freezes in the winter and thaws in the spring and how the right foundation will keep the building from moving with it, causing pipes to burst and cracks to form along the edges, among other problems.

When I look at my life in this way, something strikes me: I think we're in such a hurry to fix our issues that we avoid doing the work it takes to tackle our deeper insecurities. It's as if we want to step right into some marvelous purpose without preparing our hearts for it first. In this world that's full of instant gratification and hustle, I know I can be quick to build up an image externally, without first preparing my heart internally. It's as if I want to *appear* confident instead of actually doing the work it takes to *become* confident. And that's just laziness, honestly.

Sister, we've got to be brave enough to deal with the dirt in our lives—not by covering it up but by digging right into it. We've got to stop the surface-level show we put on to prove ourselves. That only tears down our confidence, eats away at our faith, and distracts us from the life we're made for.

If you want to break through barriers, you've got to break ground. In other words, if you want to build something beautiful with your one wild and magnificent life, you've got to go beneath the surface. You've got to start in the heart.

Take Responsibility

I'm not sitting here pretending I'm over every insecurity that flares up. I'm not saying the pressure doesn't swell beneath the surface from time to time. I'm a human on this journey to uncovering raw confidence and real purpose before I figure it all out. What I am saying, though, is that I have learned how to own up to my insecurities instead of constantly covering them up.

Owning up to them means I stop passing off responsibility for dealing with and tackling them from the inside. I'm not just talking about my insecurity with acne either. I'm talking about my insecurity as a wife. I'm talking about my insecurity when it comes to publishing this book. I'm talking about every insecurity because each one is more than skin deep.

When these thoughts creep up, I have to remind myself to pause and get to what is really behind them. What's the *systemic* issue causing that flare-up of insecurity, and why am I spending so much time picking at it instead of actually getting to the root of it?

One of the root issues of my cystic acne was too much sugar intake. To address that, I had to discipline myself to drastically cut down on sugar for a few months. That was hard but so incredibly worth it. The root issue of my insecurities as a wife is inexperience, so I have to learn how to embrace that and be willing to learn, ask questions, and do what it takes to grow. The root issue of my fear of what you think of this book, dear reader friend, is a need for affirmation. That means I have to deal with the deeper issue, not just dress up my external image. I have to ask myself *Why do I need a stranger's affirmation?* or

Why is that such a focus of mine lately? if I ever hope to take responsibility for and get rid of that insecurity. And so do you.

Own up to your insecurities. Acknowledge they exist, and then take action for how you'll deal with them at the root. They may be caused by someone else who cut you down or pointed them out, but guess what? You get to take responsibility for how you'll respond.

We live in a world full of cover-up and image maintenance and blame passing. As a result, many people are so stuck in the image they portray that they actually lose themselves in the process. I know because I've done it. But as I've learned how to treat something like acne from the inside out, it's also occurred to me that maybe if you and I—even for just a second—stood up to own our issues, stopped letting them bully us, and identified their actual cause, we might make some forward progress. In fact, we might make a bigger impact because somewhere out there in each of our spheres of influence, a little girl or young woman is hiding behind the image she made up and portrays to the world.

I don't know about you, but I don't want to be the reason another teenage girl or young woman thinks she has to live behind a made-up version of herself, hide behind labels, or live with the fear of how she might be judged if she were true to herself. I want to be the reason she learns to take off the mask and make an impact. But guess what? That requires that I remove my mask and take responsibility for my own insecurities first.

Go Deeper

I'd love to tell you my face has cleared up beautifully and I'm more confident than ever as a result of that, but guess what? That would be a lie. I *am* more confident than ever, but not because my face is magically flawless.

My confidence comes from doing the hard work to heal my acne while simultaneously doing some "heart work" too. As I've been working on making healthy changes over the last year, I've noticed improvements in my skin, but more important, I've noticed improvements in my mind-set toward this whole issue.

So, yes, it would be a lie to say I'm more confident because my skin is flawless now. Instead, as I've wrestled through this process, I've had to learn to be confident because my skin is *not* flawless now.

What courage is there in having confidence by achieving an image of perfection? I'm not saying I'm totally over every insecurity I have. News flash: I'm a human. However, I am willing to get up and fight the lies that tell me to hide the flaws, because hiding them only hurts me worse.

Maybe you don't have acne scars, but maybe you have stretch marks or cellulite or soul scars or something else this world has deemed imperfect—the very things that make you, well, you.

Don't you get it? Your purpose begins with being 100 percent you—you showing up every single day in spite of the things you believe disqualify you from trying. This starts with the stuff inside you and the raw and real you, not the fluff on the outside of the puffed-up version of you. Not you plus all your decorations. Not you plus the guy who swipes right on Tinder, or you plus the car you drive, or you plus how much weight you've lost, or you plus whatever other label you've Gorilla Glued onto your image to cover up your imperfections.

It begins with getting into the nitty-gritty parts of your heart. It starts with those parts of you that you've ignored, covered up, and accepted as your reality because you're too dang stubborn to take the mask off and ask for help—from God, from your mom, from a professional, or from all of the above.

I believe purpose begins with taking responsibility and dealing with the dirt on the inside—the lies you believe and the toxic things you say to yourself—before caking on the stuff that you think makes you more confident on the outside.

So here's my simple challenge to put raw confidence that comes from the inside, not from your image, into action: for thirty days, make it your mission to stop picking yourself apart in front of other women. Actually, just stop picking yourself apart, period. Don't call yourself fat. Don't point out your flaws in every photo you take with your friends. That is no way to talk to yourself, sister. If you wouldn't say it to your friend, don't say it to yourself.

I'll repeat that just in case you haven't had your coffee yet today: *if you wouldn't say it to your friend, don't say it to yourself.*

I mean, if Brittany's arm didn't look perfectly toned in a photo, would you point it out? No, you wouldn't. If Mary tried to make a joke at dinner but totally bombed it and made the whole table feel awkward, would you sit there and tell her how dumb that comment was and how she's just not funny and shouldn't try? I sure hope not. If you would, you seriously need to reconsider how you treat people.

Thirty days of not picking yourself apart, sister. If your arm looks flabby in that picture this Friday night, let it be and don't make a big stink about it. Are there not more important things to worry about in life?

Your thirty days start now. Every time you're about to cut yourself down or cover up or compensate to trick yourself into feeling more confident, pause and ask yourself these questions:

- *What is the root cause of this feeling?*
- *What is actually driving this?*
- *Would I say what I am thinking about myself to my friend?*

Take responsibility for your insecurity and be brave enough to go deeper and let God work inside you instead of obsessing over how you are perceived on the outside. This is where the confidence it takes to break through the pressure to prove and live your purpose starts: with you.

Part 2

Getting Unstuck

4

Overcoming Impostor Syndrome with Intentional Action Steps

D o you ever feel as if you're not who people think you are? That if people discovered who you really are, they would think you're a fraud? This phenomenon has a name: impostor syndrome.

I've struggled with it more times than I can count.

In fact, I'm even struggling with it a bit right now.

To be honest, it feels funny writing a book that you, an actual human being, will hold and read. It feels funny because I don't have years of qualifications or experience as an author. In fact, I never even dreamed of writing a book.

Interestingly, Nana wrote me a letter when I was eleven,

and in it she said, "I predict one day you will write a book. You will get to share your experiences with the world." I told you that woman dared me to dream. She knew it and believed in this all along, before I would have thought it possible. Me? Not so much. I mean, who would have thought that the girl who asked her parents to legally change her name to Sparkles would write a book? (Can we just take a moment to imagine Sparkles Lee Dooley on the cover? Thank you, Mom, for making me settle for a temporary nickname instead of a legal name change, as my six-year-old self often requested.)

Anyway, it pains me that Nana is no longer alive to read these words or hold this book in her hands, but I know that she's been with me through the process, that her heart is woven through these pages, and I wholeheartedly believe she's smiling from heaven.

Like I said, I didn't set out to write a book. In fact, my current career, this book included, began with an unlikely combination of a fancy interview, some unexpected but awesome advice from Mom, a Sharpie marker, and a little help from my friends. Seriously.

During my junior year of college, while getting a degree I was not at all passionate about, I had an interview for a summer internship with an insurance company. I interviewed in a corporate office with a bunch of men in tidy business suits; the office was without a speck of dust and filled with a lemon Pledge kind of scent.

As I sat across from executives at a big desk and answered question after question, I never felt so stiff and awkward in my whole life. I realized right then that this was so not my style. Ironically, I thought it would be. I had always envisioned myself as a successful career woman in a corporate setting, leading a team within a company and wearing pants suits because the ones I'd see on mannequins at the mall looked sophisticated.

As the interview concluded, the men stood up to shake my hand and told me they were impressed and would be in touch. The interview went fabulously, without a hitch really, and I should have been thrilled. Yet I made my way to the elevator feeling so disheartened.

This is what you've been working toward, J. This is what you want, I tried to convince myself as the elevator doors closed and I made my way down to the lobby.

I couldn't quell the unsettled feeling in my heart that day. On the drive home I began to wonder, *Did I choose the wrong thing? What if I'm not supposed to be doing this with my life? It's too late to change my major; I graduate next year! God, what is Your plan?*

Later that week my mom happened to come visit me in Bloomington, my beloved little college town in Indiana. I told her the concerns I was having. "I don't know if I want to do this corporate internship, Mom. I know I've been studying this subject and it's important to my future, but I just can't get myself excited about it!"

I expected Mom to remind me how much time and money had been invested in the pursuit of my degree, or how great an opportunity this was, or how I ought to at least give it a shot. Except she didn't do that. She simply responded, "Okay, so don't. Don't do it."

Wait . . . what? Don't? Isn't telling your kid not to take a job opportunity against some unwritten mom code?

"What do you mean, *don't*?" I asked.

"Don't feel the pressure to prove yourself or think you have to figure it all out this second. For now I encourage you to try some other stuff while you're still in school."

Don't take the job? Try some stuff? What is this baloney?

Again I asked what she meant.

"You work hard and have done everything to be responsible with school, future opportunities, and more. Maybe you'll get the internship; maybe you won't. And I'm proud of you regardless," she explained. "But I think you've put so much pressure on yourself to have the perfect plan that you haven't taken any time to explore your personal interests and passions along the way."

I did not see that coming.

However, in that moment I realized all the career-related expectations I thought my parents had of me were just *perceived* expectations.

Honestly, I had no idea what I wanted to do. I was never one of those lucky ones who woke up when she was seven years old thinking, *I'm positive I want to be a doctor!* and then never lost that passion all the way through graduation from med school.

If that's your story, more power to you, sis. But it's not mine. I'm the definition of a girl who is learning as she goes, figuring out how to trust that God has a plan, all while having wacky unfigured-out dreams in my head.

So I began to explore some stuff that interested me.

Among many different things, hand-lettering became something I really enjoyed. It was therapeutic for a stressed-out college student. I would letter quotes that inspired me, Bible verses that influenced me, and pretty much anything else I wanted to remember. Writing something down carefully and beautifully made it more meaningful to me.

After some time, Matt, my boyfriend who would eventually become my husband, noticed I was creating all these little designs on napkins and in notebooks. One day he said, "You know, J, you're pretty good at that, and it seems like a really great creative outlet for you during stressful weeks of school. You should start an Etsy store or something!"

I had only vaguely heard of Etsy, an emerging online marketplace to sell handcrafted items.

Curious, I decided to create an account and try it out. Unsure if this would even work, my first few pieces were pretty primitive. Seriously, I thought it would be a good idea to letter a quote with a Sharpie on a piece of *computer paper* (professional, right?) and then take it down to the dungeon-like art room in the sorority house and take photos of it to post online.

I doubted whether it'd sell, but then one day, while sitting at my desk, I got an email notifying me that a lady in Texas bought my item! I leaped out of my chair. "Oh my gosh! Are you serious? I made my first sale!"

There really is nothing like creating something and making your first-ever sale. *Whoa. I made something with my hands. And somebody likes it . . . enough to pay money for it. Is this real?*

Of course, then I had to figure out how to package and ship it properly so it wouldn't get bent.

From that day on, my little lettering business grew. I made an account to share my designs on social media, and every week the orders increased. For a while I did everything on my own. I would buy blank items (canvases, mugs . . . *not* computer paper!), draw a design on them, photograph them, and upload them to Etsy. Once they sold, I would print labels, package the items, drive Nana's old hand-me-down Nissan Altima to the post office to drop my packages off, and then manage to squeeze in a little studying before bed.

Truth be told, I felt like such an impostor as I'd answer customer service emails from the biology class I probably should have been paying attention to. To this day I can't tell you the first thing about a cell nucleus, but I can rattle off a billion facts about return slips and postage rates.

Day after day I'd do this. Finally it dawned on me that I needed to do two things: first, learn how to have my designs printed on items so I wouldn't have to do it all by hand; and second, ask for help.

As the volume of orders grew, I began to recruit my friends and roommates to help me package, promising to pay them in pizza. They agreed without needing much more convincing. Turns out when you bribe college students with free food, they're much more likely to oblige.

Okay, I'm totally kidding. They offered to help simply because they supported and believed in my crazy ideas. For that I'll be forever grateful. Little did any of us know that those small beginnings would lead to so much more.

We'd sit upstairs on the third-floor storage closet floor, shoving packing peanuts into boxes, and talk and laugh for hours on end. Many of the lessons and advice we'd trade in those conversations inspired me, so I would write about them in social media captions.

I quickly learned that those stories resonated with women around the world, not just the girls in AOII's third-floor storage closet. Some of the articles I'd post alongside photos of my lettering designs picked up steam, some getting thousands of shares on Facebook.

Within a year or so, I had a growing online community (something I didn't even know was possible at the time). And they were following me for my writing and content more than for my lettering business. Again I began to feel insecure.

It was crazy to think that women with ten times more life experience were following a twenty-one-year-old sorority girl who hadn't yet finished college. At that time, I rarely shared photos of myself, so I don't think they realized how young I was. I often tried to act older and more sophisticated because I was convinced that if people found out my age, they'd unfollow me and perhaps even ask to return anything they bought from my shop.

That may sound dramatic, but impostor syndrome can take over when our insecurities combine with the expectations we perceive others have of us, together creating a massive pressure to prove ourselves.

Looking back, I now realize that I will always feel like an impostor when I live under the pressure to prove myself instead of just living intentionally, before I prove anything.

Never in a billion years did I anticipate doing this with my

life. I was just "trying stuff," like Mom suggested. But just trying stuff turned into a small shop, which grew into writing a
blog and eventually speaking. It also led to trying other creative
endeavors like a photography business on the side, raising
money for causes I believed in, creating online courses, hosting
a podcast, and now writing a book.

Have there been a thousand times I've felt unqualified
along the way? Yup. Were there things I really messed up? More
than I can count. Did I accidentally almost put us into debt my
first year of marriage? Guilty. Was I threatened to be sued for a
mistake? Actually, yes, and that was traumatizing. (Shout out to
my dad for walking me through that one.) Have I embarrassed
myself? You bet. Did I rewrite this book three times before
publishing it? Also yes.

Sister, so many things have gone wrong since the start of
this journey, but I think that's what has made it so right too.
Every step has been worth it, and every step from here forward
will be worth it.

I didn't wake up one day with everything figured out. I
didn't just happen upon my purpose. I fumbled into projects I
found interesting, and slowly over time—as I battled my struggle with impostor syndrome and the unnecessary pressure to
figure out my dreams—I learned something powerful and
humbling.

My purpose wasn't in that first Etsy sale. It wasn't tied up in how many packages I could sell or in how much I got paid or even in how many people read my captions. It wasn't something I found when signing a book contract or stepping onto a stage. It has never had anything to do with my position—in an internship, in a sorority, or as a small-business owner. It's not even in this book or as an author. Instead, it has had everything to do with the passion and purpose I bring to whatever space I occupy in my everyday life, labels aside.

Honestly, my own unfigured-out dreams and Mom's encouragement to explore and experiment have probably made me look like a crazy person over the years with everything I've tried. I don't fit in just one box, because I've refused to let labels continue to define me.

So, yes, I might look like a crazy person who doesn't know what she's doing with her life. And sometimes I have to chuckle and remember that's not entirely untrue. (I mean, do any of us really know exactly what we're doing with our lives? No.)

Maybe a meaningful life is not at all about figuring it out but rather just being willing to get outside our comfort zones.

Remember, none of this happened because I woke up one day and had a crystal-clear dream that I went after. None of this happened because I was an expert at anything. All this happened because Mom gave me permission to do something I'd never once considered doing: to explore and experiment before I had a perfect plan to execute. And it happened because I decided to just go for it even before I knew what "it" would become.

Now, I want to emphasize that Mom didn't tell me to drop out of school and just do what I like. She encouraged me to learn alongside and grow beyond what I was currently doing, without dropping my responsibilities. That said, please do not read this and just quit your boring job tomorrow, saying you're taking my mom's advice. (If you do that, you're probably going to end up eating ramen for a few weeks and resenting me.) There's wisdom in planning if you're going to make a big move like that.

Just as Mom encouraged me to explore—to open doors I didn't even know existed—while I stewarded my academic responsibilities, I also encourage you to try some things that bring you life and joy, even if they don't directly correlate with your career or obligations in this season.

I say this because I think so many of us put far too much pressure on ourselves to strike gold on the first step we take or the first thing we try, and when that doesn't turn out to be so great, we are hesitant to try again. So few of us allow ourselves to try new things, because we convince ourselves we shouldn't for one reason or another.

I want to look at some of the reasons I have struggled to

dream outside the box or try new things, because I have a feeling you might have similar excuses—I mean, "reasons."

Why We Don't "Try Stuff" or Dream Outside the Box

1. Expectations

Before I talked to Mom, I thought she expected me to do a certain thing with my life, something that was secure, stable, and successful from the perspective of society. However, I realized how wrong I was. If we hadn't had that conversation, I might never have tried something outside the qualifications on my résumé. I'm aware that not everyone has that luxury, and perhaps your parents or spouse or someone else really does have unrealistic expectations of you. Even so, only *you* get to decide if those expectations will control you.

Even if others don't impose expectations on us, I believe that when our own expectations of how our life should go don't match our reality, we begin to make excuses. At least, I know I have. Our own unmet expectations can hold us back from stepping into new things as we attempt to avoid further disappointment. Have you ever let this happen? Are you letting it happen now? Knock that off, okay? It's not helping anyone, especially you. You haven't lost your purpose just because you missed an opportunity or failed on your first try.

2. Opinions

So many of us don't try anything outside our comfort zones and qualifications because we are concerned with how other people will perceive it. When we run into Great-Aunt Mildred at the family reunion and she asks, "So what do you do?" most of us want to be able to give a short and sweet answer that will satisfy the question and also make us appear successful. When our passions and roles don't quite fit into a particular label or aren't even entirely clear to us, insecurity sets in.

I think we cling to labels more than we realize because labels give us something to quickly impress others with. Replying with "I'm an accountant" will probably make Great-Aunt Mildred smile and nod in approval. However, responding with "I'm trying some different things, dreaming up a nonprofit, working on my master's, and barista-ing on the side" might make her raise her eyebrows in concern. She might not understand, and her reaction has the potential to make us rethink our entire lives.

3. Boxes or Labels

My mom once said, "Women tend to put themselves in boxes." Think about how true that is. How often do you see a woman you know and immediately associate a couple of words with her name based on what she *does*, subconsciously labeling her accordingly? How often do you do this to yourself? We so often assign labels based on one component of someone's life, even if unintentionally. *She's the photographer. She's the dentist. She's the stay-at-home mom. She's the smart girl. She's the fitness guru.* The problem with doing this to others is that, yes, although she may be the smart girl, that's not all she is, right? We've put her in a box based on one thing we perceive. As a result, we end up assuming we must fit into the box we perceive others have put us in.

This makes it really difficult to try something new, because we've basically believed we are what we do. How do we break out of this? We can try two things. First, we can take small steps and make incremental changes when we sense it's time to pivot. Second, we have to get comfortable with surprising and even disappointing people at times.

A really small personal example is when people would come up to me and say, "Oh, you're SoulScripts (the name of my shop)!" It began to make me cringe. I wanted to say, "No, I'm Jordan! I'm so much more than that. I don't want to be pigeonholed to that!" Even though SoulScripts is a brand I started, it began to feel as though it were permanently branded on me too, marking my entire identity. So one day I decided to make a change that felt like a tiny step in the right direction to diminishing labels and expectations: I changed my social media from the shop to my name. It might seem trivial, but at the time it felt like a huge risk in the right direction. And isn't that basically what an unknown step of faith is?

So what about you? Start envisioning your life as a path to walk on, not as a box to sit in. That simple mind-set shift will help you keep moving forward into unknown (but often exciting) places instead of remaining stuck, stagnant, and comfortable.

4. The Risk of Embarrassment

I believe we also hesitate to step into new opportunities, ideas, or interests because we don't want people to see us starting small or to see us fail if things don't work out. When we try new things, we have to start small most of the time. I didn't start speaking at huge events. I started speaking at small events, usually in rooms without a stage, and every single time I felt like such a fraud.

When I finally did get to speak at a larger event, I was the girl who missed my cue and walked out on stage at the wrong time without even realizing it. Seriously, I just started talking, completely unaware that the band wasn't done with their set and that I was not supposed to be on center stage. When I realized the sound guy had shut my mic off and no one could hear me, I looked around to see everyone staring at me with wide eyes. I could feel their embarrassment for me as my cheeks flushed red and I awkwardly curtseyed and hustled off the stage. With my confidence level registering a big fat zero, I wanted nothing more than to go hide in a cave somewhere for the rest of my life.

After the event, though, a young girl came up to me and said, "Thank you for being awkward. It reminds me that the people on stage are human like me." *What?* Isn't that something? My embarrassment actually encouraged a young girl. And I realized for the first time that maybe embarrassment can be an unexpected form of empowerment. My advice? Shift the way you see embarrassment. It's no roadblock. It's dynamite to blast you beyond the confines of the walls your pride puts up.

Tips for Overcoming Impostor Syndrome

Before I wrap up this chapter, I want to share a few lessons I've learned about overcoming impostor syndrome. If you've ever felt like a fraud, seen yourself as unqualified, struggled to believe God has a plan for you, or said, "SOS! I have no idea what I'm doing," listen up because this is important.

1. Ask More Questions and Be Coachable

When you begin to feel unqualified or like an impostor, it's so much better to admit that you're not sure and ask for help instead of trying to mask it and act as if you know what you're doing. This takes away the pressure to have it all figured out and gives you freedom to learn, grow, and figure it out as you go.

2. Embrace Your Reality and Start Where You Are

Whenever I've felt insecure about my age or my lack of experience or anything else, I've found that it helps to look inward to see where that insecurity is coming from. I focus on what I am equipped to do instead of looking at everyone else and becoming frustrated by what I'm unable to do. Trust me, this is far more effective.

There will always be someone who has a little bit more figured out than I do. There will always be someone a little older, a little smarter, a little cuter, or a little funnier. But if I can learn to look past that and appreciate where I am, I'll be able to show up and make an impact. I'll be able to embrace my place and run my race. My advice? Stop focusing on what you don't know or don't have and start focusing on what you do have right now—even if that's only a Sharpie marker and a piece of computer paper.

3. Be Prepared to Fail

Many people will tell you to expect failure, but they'll stop right there. What good is it to expect something if you aren't prepared to handle it? If the meteorologist tells me to expect a blizzard and I don't prepare by turning the heat up in my house or changing my travel plans or salting my driveway before it hits, that blizzard is going to have a much worse effect on my life than it would've if I had prepared for it.

So don't merely expect failure but actually prepare for how you will respond when it comes. Yes, have faith that it will work out if it's the good Lord's will. However, don't be shocked if it doesn't work out the way you think it might. Instead of reacting to an unwanted error or failure, consider how you'll respond if what you're trying doesn't go according to plan.

4. Shift Your Perspective on Failure

To piggyback off point number three, we need to stop using the word *failure* so much. Unless you refuse to try or just quit being willing to grow, then no matter how bad it is, it's not failure; it's learning. You don't overcome impostor syndrome by having some superpower-status immunity to mistakes or by being a know-it-all. You overcome impostor syndrome and unfigured-out dreams by learning. If you're always looking at mess-ups as learning experiences, you will never fail. You will just learn. When we learn, we grow.

5. Execute Incremental, Implementable Imperfection Action

When I started lettering, I didn't have a five-year business plan. In fact, it overwhelmed me to even think about that. If I had put the pressure on myself to have it all figured out in the infancy of the business, I probably wouldn't have even given it a go. However, I could take a first step by learning about and starting an Etsy account. I could take a second step by going to Hobby Lobby and picking up some canvases and paint. I could take a third step by ordering packing peanuts online and then a fourth by asking my friends for help.

Take the pressure off, sis. Nothing you try, nothing you put your hand to—whether it's med school, making your own small business, or mothering—will be an overnight production. There's wisdom in planning. But if it comes down to either figuring it all out or just digging deep down inside yourself and taking a baby step toward beginning, I vote for the latter option. Because big steps are really just the result of incremental decisions implemented imperfectly, one at a time.

Allow Yourself to Dream

Sister, you will tackle your unfigured-out dreams only when you give yourself permission to dream outside the box. Just try some stuff and show up as your full self, not an older version or more figured-out version. Don't try to be the person you perceive others expect you to be. Be you, with your wild ideas and funny quirks and unfigured-out dreams and lack of expertise. When you do that, when you root yourself in faith and step beyond the labels you may be wrapped up in, something divine happens. You may even fumble into a dream you didn't know you had.

Friend, try stuff before it makes sense, because it doesn't need to all make sense in order for God to use it. He's got this. He's got you. And that means you can do something as seemingly small as doodling on computer paper with no idea what it could turn into, even *before* the lady in Texas makes her purchase. And still be living your purpose.

5

Overcoming Disappointment with a Different Perspective

Perhaps something worse than working our way through unfigured-out dreams and impostor syndrome is having our seemingly figured-out dreams crushed. Especially the ones we've worked our butts off for. The result here is disappointment, which can be debilitating. Disappointment can create additional obstacles like doubt, discouragement, anxiety, and frustration.

When we feel let down, or as though our plans have shattered, getting back up can be as hard as trying to clear a hurdle with a bum ankle. Personally, when some aspect of my life doesn't work out according to plan, I tend to stress out, and at times I've let failure and disappointment sideline me instead of firing me up to get back in the game.

This is kind of how my husband and I felt when we thought we had a plan when we were dating in college. We were convinced Matt's football platform would be key to living out our purpose. But when that platform disappeared, which initially felt like a major setback, we learned some super valuable life lessons that I'm going to share with you.

First, I'll give you a little context. Matt and I met at Indiana University when he was a junior and I was a sophomore, right around the time I joined AOII. Originally from Arizona, he came all the way to good ole Indiana because of a football scholarship. Although he was a devilishly handsome, insanely talented athlete, I was floored by his humility, faith, and breadth of wisdom.

We were neighbors on campus and had mutual friends, and we met on a Wednesday night in November. We sat on the old hand-me-down couch inside apartment E3 and talked for hours, telling stories about our families, discovering beliefs and interests we had in common, and sharing our dreams for the future.

To this day, we say it was as if our hearts were old friends even though we were meeting for the very first time. During that conversation Matt mentioned he had dreams of playing in the National Football League after graduation.

"Oh, cool," I said casually with a shoulder shrug, trying not to come off like a fan girl.

After that first meeting Matt asked me on an official date,

and over time our relationship became more and more serious. I always loved wearing his practice jersey on game day. It was like a privilege to me to walk around campus and represent Matt Dooley, number 91, with pride.

The longer we dated, the more I was exposed to the life of an athlete: practices at five in the morning, two-a-days (practice twice a day), agents, contracts, drug tests, playbooks, film, more film, special diets, and more. As we began to talk about marriage and as he trained for the upcoming draft, I realized his pursuit of the NFL dream would inevitably be part of our journey together.

A part of me found the opportunity exciting. It was fun to cheer him on from the sidelines, help him decide on the best agent, and be part of the preparation and process. On the other hand, I found it all a little nerve racking. This wasn't one of those situations where a clear plan was possible. We had endless unknowns and possibilities and very few certainties.

Still, we had so much hope that it would work out the way we wanted. Several NFL scouts complimented Matt at his pro day, and he was nationally ranked among the top five in his class at his position. On top of that, his agent seemed sure he would be a shoo-in.

I should probably mention that when pursuing something like the NFL, a man must put nearly all his eggs in one basket. Any wise adviser will tell you that's never a smart move in life, but when it comes to something as big and elite as the NFL, you can't afford to give it only 75 percent of your focus. Unlike other college seniors, you can't be spending time looking for a backup job. You've got to be zeroed in. It's all or nothing.

The spring before draft day, Matt left campus and moved to a nearby city to train full time for six weeks. One time when I visited him, he showed me the fancy big facility where he trained each day. Then he introduced me to the guys he was working with—some of whom went on to become first- and second-round draft picks.

It was all so exciting, so elite.

Draft day rolled around, and we invited a bunch of friends over for a little party. We wanted to celebrate with our people when Matt got the call!

Since he was a long snapper, a specialist position, Matt expected to be signed as a free agent. A free agent is an undrafted player that teams choose as soon as the seven draft rounds end. Based on what pros in the league had told him, teams would start to call just a few minutes after the seventh round ended. Matt would have to pick the team where he had the greatest shot at beating out the veteran long snapper and therefore making the final roster in the fall.

He asked me to be with him when the calls came in so I could jot down notes for him to relay to his agent before making a final decision. We were ready. While our friends waited in the living room, I sat with Matt, holding the special pad of paper and pen for this very moment. He sat with his hands folded, anxiously picking at his thumbnail, eagerly waiting for the phone to ring. We were so excited for the next step in our journey to reveal itself.

Five minutes passed, and the only sound in the hollow air was the ticking of the wall clock. *No sweat, right?*

Ten minutes passed. *Maybe they're just busy?*

Fifteen minutes. His agent called. The Minnesota Vikings had called to express interest but made no offer. *A good sign but not quite what we need.*

Twenty-five minutes passed. *Can they get through? Maybe we don't have good cell service?*

Thirty long minutes. *Still nothing.*

Forty minutes. His brow furrowed, Matt started to sweat, saying, "Something's wrong! This is taking too long!"

The minutes dragged on, and each one seemed longer than the last.

Text messages poured in from family and friends: "Anything yet?" and "Where are you heading, Matt?"

Forty-five minutes passed. Other free agents and draft picks started announcing their new homes online. One friend was heading to Atlanta, and another was packing his bags for Kansas City.

At the one-hour mark, the phone was still silent. We walked

into the living room to see our friends, who were still anticipating good news and ready to celebrate. Their expressions changed the moment they saw the disappointment on our faces. It didn't make any sense. Matt's agent didn't have any answers either. He seemed just as confused as we were.

We tried to piece it together, but we couldn't come up with an answer. We were stuck—and without a backup plan.

Anxious for Answers

It was no easy thing to witness the love of my life's plans and perceived purpose seem to evaporate before his eyes. That day I felt the sting for Matt—the sting of disappointment that comes with broken dreams and shattered plans, especially without an explanation. And honestly, it stung me too. Even though I wasn't the one on the field, it felt as though we'd been chasing that dream together with how involved I'd been and how much we'd planned a future together.

Maybe you've experienced deep disappointment or put years of work toward a big dream only to fail. Maybe you've been laid flat on your back or seen the opportunity you've worked so hard for stolen from you without reason. Maybe plans you made or a purpose you thought was certain shattered within seconds, and you couldn't understand why.

That confusing, disappointing night, Matt held it together.

I, on the other hand, cried my eyes out. I was so ready for him to take that next step, to start living what we thought was the next piece of the purpose puzzle. Instead, it felt as though our whole plan had crumbled into a messy heap of missed opportunities and misplaced dreams. I hurt for him. I hurt for us. I ached with disappointment and felt anxious for answers.

What do you do when everything you thought you wanted crumbles? When your dreams now seem out of reach and the purpose you thought was yours is completely obscured?

Maybe you do what I do: search for answers. Isn't that what we all do? Crave reasons, explanations, and direction?

Why did this happen?

What should I do next?

How can I fix this?

When we don't get those answers right away, it hurts, and sometimes it hinders our steps forward. We long for clarity, but perhaps true purpose requires closeness with God. When I get impatient, however, I trade closeness for clarity, just when He's daring me to press in and trust there's a bigger plan.

By that fall Matt had some tryouts, but he still hadn't been signed. Hope was dwindling, and he began to search for an entry-level job since it didn't look as if he'd be getting called anytime soon.

Later that year, while working for a medical device company, he got a call out of the blue. The Pittsburgh Steelers were bringing him in for a workout. We were excited, but we didn't tell anyone. We didn't want to get our families' and friends' hopes up only to have to break disappointing news again. But after Matt's workout it happened.

They signed him! I squealed and jumped up and down when he called to tell me, because I couldn't contain my excitement. He had finally made it! He was added to the preseason roster and given the number 42 jersey. It was official.

We'd been engaged for almost six months at that point, and we'd changed our wedding date multiple times because of his ever-fluctuating career plans. Now, finally, the year of uncertainty was coming to an end. It was happening. The dream was coming true! Or so we thought.

Throughout the spring and summer months, Matt lived in Pittsburgh, training and practicing, working hard to secure a spot on the final roster. I lived with my parents and planned our wedding, now scheduled for Labor Day weekend—close, we soon found out, to when teams make final roster cuts. But it was too late to change the wedding date again. Nope, that wasn't stressful at all. (That's a lie.)

I believe I prayed harder in those few months than I ever had in my whole life, clinging to the hope that Matt would make it, that he'd still have a job in the NFL when we got married.

I know you might be thinking, *What's the big deal? Even*

if he got cut, didn't he make like a kajillion dollars when he signed? Pause right there, sister, because that's not at all the truth. Allow me to offer you a peek behind the curtain. What most people don't realize about NFL free agents is that most of them don't make their "big money" salary until they're added to the final roster. Until the preseason ends and the season starts, they don't earn much. We still laugh at the fact that Matt took a pay cut to sign with the Steelers. As a free agent rookie, he didn't have a signing bonus and his weekly stipend was barely enough to cover his bills. I was working part time but hadn't started a full-time career because we hoped I would be moving to Pittsburgh with him in the fall.

My income wasn't enough to support both of us, and he didn't have savings to get us through if he was released from the team. We had no plan B. Our livelihood was dependent on him surviving all the rounds of cuts he would face in August. One morning just thirteen days before the wedding day, Mom and I were reviewing RSVPs when my phone chimed, notifying me of a text message. I expected a "good morning" from my Steeler, just as I got every morning.

After I grabbed the phone, I saw three little words that changed everything. Three words that made my heart sink. Three words I never wanted to read: "Just got released."

That's it. That's all he said. I didn't know whether to cry or curl up in a ball or both. Crushed dreams, round number two.

I was worried. I was upset. And again I wanted answers I knew I'd probably never get. Why did this happen after he had worked so hard? Why did his efforts keep ending in disappointment?

We were getting married in thirteen days, and we didn't know where we'd live, where we'd be working, or how we'd make ends meet. *Great.*

How do you move forward when you get the news you prayed against? When plan A crumbles and you have no plan B? When you're about to step into a new season of life with zero sense of security and no idea what will happen next?

A couple of weeks later, we said our vows in a tiny white chapel and walked back down the aisle as husband and wife, without a plan beyond that day. As family and friends threw rice in our hair and we stepped into the old Studebaker getaway car, I had this overwhelming feeling of excitement that comes when you say yes to someone or something you love before anything else is figured out.

And I learned that big steps forward before you figure it all out are simple, terrifying, and beautiful all at once. Perhaps a little risk like that is what makes life so fun, so worth living, after all.

In those first few months, we fumbled our way through the most insecure season of our lives, longing for answers but often left with uncertainty. I began to wonder if maybe God doesn't give us answers because He dares us to spend less time trying to figure out what we're doing and more time having faith in what He's doing. Perhaps the broken pieces that come with disappointment, frustration, and failure prepare us for a purpose we couldn't have dreamed up on our own. Maybe they're the very things we need.

Key Lessons We Had to Learn

Not long ago, I received a text message that rocked me to the core: "The most important lessons are the hardest to learn."

I hadn't heard something truer in a long time. The most important lessons are the ones we can't afford to miss, the ones we learn in the most challenging, disappointing, or downright discouraging situations in life. Our pursuit of the NFL didn't go the way we planned or hoped, but that doesn't mean that our life turned out any less wonderful or that it lacked the purpose it would have had if this dream had worked out long term.

Those uncertain years held a lot of frustration, but they also taught me so much about living a meaningful (not just happy or comfortable) life. If you feel as if shattered plans, broken dreams, failures, or disappointments have robbed you of your purpose, may I take your hand and whisper a couple of crucial lessons I had to learn?

1. Shift Your Mind-Set

Sure, we didn't make enough money to support ourselves from Matt's short-lived NFL career, there were often more disappointments than dreams come true, and he certainly didn't get as far as he would have liked. However, we had to stop saying it didn't work out . . . because it actually did. We had to shift our entire mind-set from "that was a bummer" to "that was a blessing" as we realized that it did, in fact, work out exactly how it was supposed to, even if it wasn't how we wanted it to.

Did we have to take time to process the disappointment? Of course. There's wisdom in allowing yourself to feel what you're feeling. But if you look at every disappointment in life as an obstacle instead of an opportunity, you will become a wallower. Wallowers get swallowed up by life instead of making the most of life.

I often remember what my dad always said when I needed to tackle something with wisdom instead of whining when I was growing up: "We're not raising wimps over here!"

It may sound a little harsh, but my dad is a jovial kind of guy. He says everything with a big grin and a positive attitude. So when he reminds me that he didn't raise me to be a wimp, that doesn't mean he raised me not to feel or struggle. He's always given me room to process emotions and wrestle through life. But that's just it—he's given me room to wrestle with life but never encouraged me to back down and let life's challenges win. When he reminds me that I'm no wimp, he's reminding me that I don't have to give life's disappointments the power to beat me up. I can't always avoid getting punched by life, but I can decide if I'll punch back with purpose. And so can you.

2. Don't Trust the Process

When it came to the ups and downs of the NFL, so many people told us to "just trust the process; it'll work out." But when the process didn't work out and proved to be completely unreliable, Matt and I learned we had to stop trusting the NFL, or whatever dream we might have had, because that is a weak god that will let us down ten times out of ten. We had to stop trusting the process because the process is full of potholes and pitfalls. We had to instead start trusting God in the process.

Worry and insecurity lose their grip when I come to grips with the fact that I'm not in control (no matter how many prayers I pray) and that I can't trust anything outside of God. I cannot control what happens to me. I can only choose how I respond to what happens. The same goes for you. The only thing you can control is your response when your best-laid plans crumble. You can choose to place your faith in the unsteady process or trust that a bigger purpose will always break through your plans when God has something so much better for you.

And, hey, maybe things go wrong so God can set us right.

3. Get Over the Platform

For a little while, Matt and I thought the NFL was going to be our platform, but when that platform crumbled, we realized a few things. The first was that we already had a platform in our small spheres of influence, even if it wasn't on a big stage. The second was that we don't need a big platform to live our purpose (and honestly, how prideful that kind of thinking is).

If we have one, great, but that's not where our purpose is found. Instead, we just need to love people. Purpose lies in how we show up in our spheres of influence and how people are loved by us. No platform is required for that. No big name, fancy organization, or impressive job is necessary. Showing up can be done by both the broke college student and the established entrepreneur. Instead of trying to show off, each of us can choose to show up and give what we have.

Maybe we need to fail at what we think we want so we can learn to be faithful with what we already have, right where we are. Remembering this lesson helps me keep a healthy perspective on whatever influence or platform I'm given, whether it's a local leadership position, online, or even in my small-town community.

What spheres of influence are you overlooking because you've been so focused on a sphere of influence you'd like to have? In other words, are you overlooking how you could make a positive impact on your next-door neighbor or your difficult in-law because you're so focused on the influence that getting a promotion or an award might give you?

Over the course of those two years, I learned that football wasn't the key to our purpose after all and that our purpose could not and should not be so dependent on such a temporary and unpredictable platform. Maybe that would have been one specific way to carry out our purpose, but it would not have been the purpose in and of itself.

When I get caught up in having a big platform or in feeling pressure to prove myself to people, I have to stand in front of a mirror and speak this out loud: "Focus on loving people more than on getting them to like you."

Again, remember significance over specifics. The specific roles or platforms we have are not our significance. They are places to bring our purpose to, but they are not the point of everything.

Your purpose is not your job title or career path or any other means of influence. Those are simply avenues for living out the God-given purpose you already have.

4. Develop an Attitude of Gratitude

Sister, disappointment will crush the determination and drive right out of you if you are not grateful for the experience it gave you. Grumbling will turn a letdown into a lockdown on your life. That's when you'll feel stuck. That's where I've gotten stuck before. On the flip side, gratitude can turn a letdown into a lesson that redirects the trajectory of your life from what you thought you wanted to what you're actually made for.

I don't know about you, but I don't want to be the girl who lets setbacks hold me back. I want to be the kind of woman who looks the fattest disappointments in the face and says, *You don't scare me. I'm thankful for you because you will be a lesson that will shape me into who I'll become.*

You're Not Missing Out

I think we live in a world full of people who are so afraid to miss out on something else that they completely miss out on where they actually are. FOMO is an acronym that stands for "fear of missing out," and it is a real problem. Everywhere I look, I see young people overcommitting themselves and obsessing over a perceived notion that they're somehow missing out on life if they don't go to a specific place or attend a certain social function. My brother and I were recently discussing this phenomenon, and he shared what he'd observed among peers. We talked about how it seems like so many people are dissatisfied with where they are because they're chasing after some experience they see others doing online.

Then he shook his head and said, "The carrot is a hologram."

Holy cow. He was right. It looks so real, doesn't it? The

promise that if you just move to that hip big city in your twenties, or get that job you've been working toward, or take that cool photo to post on Instagram and prove you're relevant, you'll be satisfied.

The second you grab that carrot dangling in front of you—make that move, get that job, or post the cool photo—there's no lasting satisfaction. You immediately move on to the next thing you think you're missing out on. And it never stops. The carrot is a false promise of fulfillment. It's nothing more than a hologram. Are you still believing that your dream come true will be the only thing that fills you up or that figuring out your next step will reveal your hidden purpose?

It's one thing to set goals and be diligent and intentional as we work toward them in the here and now. However, we have to keep ourselves in check because living with a fear of what we're missing out on rather than focusing on what we're currently standing on top of is toxic to our joy, our confidence, and the impact we can have right where we are.

Know what else that kind of thinking does? It sets us up to get stuck in disappointment instead of stepping forward in important directions.

When I look back at our challenging yet refining first year of marriage, I'm thankful we didn't get everything we wanted. I also realize we didn't miss out on anything we weren't meant to have in the first place. Had our plans gone how we initially hoped, we likely wouldn't have moved back to Matt's hometown and been able to spend what ended up being the last few months of his Pop-Pop's life with him. Sure, that didn't look glamorous, but guess what? Sometimes the glamorous things we go after are the most unimportant. On the flip side, sometimes the most unglamorous things we do are the most important.

On that same note, if Matt would have made the final roster that year, I might not be writing this book. It's probably not something I would have thought to pursue. If we hadn't been disappointed in that season, we wouldn't have discovered all the dreams we didn't even realize we had for this season.

Perhaps even more important, we might not have learned on such a personal level what it looks like to embrace the power of impact in unseen spaces and ordinary places. It's easy to embrace impact that is seen and applauded on big stages, but maybe the goodness is truly in the ordinary everyday.

Now whenever I catch myself feeling the pressure to do what looks impressive or am caught up in the lie that I'm somehow missing out on something, I have to center myself, check my heart, and honestly answer this question: Am I overlooking something right under my nose because I'm so preoccupied with the notion that I'm missing out?

I dare you to do the same. Maybe you haven't missed out on what really matters at all. Maybe that thing you thought you wanted is not a broken dream but a step toward a much bigger one.

Don't overlook what's in front of you because you're so fixated on what's behind you. I'm serious. There is no room for FOMO because the fear of missing out is just a perception, not a reality. If your plans didn't work out, there is a reason. You've just got to keep your eyes open wide enough to see that something new is being worked out in your life.

So if you feel as if you really messed up or missed out on your one big opportunity, please reevaluate. Get your eyes off what didn't go right and refocus for five seconds. Don't overlook the purpose and opportunity right in front of you. Get back to what really matters, not what you think you missed out on.

Because, honestly, what does a gal really gain when she gets the whole world but loses her soul?[1]

6

Overcoming Shame by Sharing

'll be honest. The scale freaked me out for a long time. It became a trigger for me since I was a kid and the doctor weighed me during a checkup and said I was in the ninetieth percentile for height and weight.

While that didn't mean that I was overweight or unhealthy or even that anything was necessarily wrong, my nine-year-old brain translated that to mean "She's a Sasquatch."

I also developed early, and it didn't help that when I was eleven, a pretty and petite girl told me I had thunder thighs or that boys asked if I stuffed my bra.

Although I was one of the biggest and tallest kids in class growing up, by high school I stopped growing so quickly and everyone caught up. Now, as an adult, I'm average when it comes to height and at a healthy weight. Still, a girl is impressionable during the first twelve years of her life, and always having to stand with the boys in the back for school pictures so all the smaller girls could be in the front made me insecure.

My point is that those lies I believed about being too big during my formative years caused me to be anything but a huge fan of my body. I've had to fight my own mind to maintain healthy habits. And, for a time, I did develop a really unhealthy relationship with food and exercise.

It all started toward the end of my freshman year of college while trying on pink bikinis for the summer. Inside the walls of the Target fitting room, a familiar insecurity set in. And I didn't like the girl I saw staring back at me in the mirror.

So I set out to get in better shape as fast as humanly possible. At the time I thought I was simply getting fit and eating well, but it's obvious to me now that it was much deeper than that. More than just being insecure, I was also reaching for control because my life had begun to spin out of control.

My good intentions to eat healthier and exercise more soon became an intense obsession with calorie counting, food restriction, and extreme exercise. Depriving myself of calories and exercising excessively led to losing many pounds unnecessarily. I grew addicted to the progress, to watching the number on the scale go down with each passing week. My face became gaunt and my energy levels plummeted. Still I pushed through.

My parents grew very concerned as they saw how dangerously thin I was getting. I kept telling them it was no big deal. I explained I was simply training for a half marathon that I planned to run in honor of Nana's passing, since it would take place on the last weekend in October—exactly one year after her death.

I thought I fooled them, but Mom didn't buy it. I later learned Mom was so concerned that she talked with a doctor to find out what to watch for or what she should do if the behavior continued. She's always been so great about watching out for me, even when I didn't know she was doing it.

The doctor first explained to her that behavior like this is usually deeper than just body image insecurities. In other words, it's not merely physical but can also be psychological. Then he asked if I had recently gone through any major life changes or overwhelming experiences. She explained to him that I was processing a handful of things all at once, from mourning the loss of Nana to adjusting to college to experiencing a breakup.

Given that information, the doctor said my extreme behavior and restriction was likely a response to those emotional challenges but might improve once I completed the half marathon.

Instead of intervening immediately, he advised her to monitor my weight and told her that if the extreme dieting and exercise continued after I completed the race, I might need to be seen.

When I went back to school that August, Mom sent me with a scale and required that I send her a photo of my weight each week. Since I was unaware of her meeting with the doctor, I was initially annoyed and tried to convince her that I was fine—that she was overreacting. Nevertheless, she persisted. And so, like clockwork, every week leading up to the half marathon, I'd send her a picture of my weight.

As the day of the race grew nearer, my behavior became even more extreme. When my college roommate texted me to ask about the stash of diet pills she found in my dresser, I immediately questioned why she'd dare snoop around in my things, completely avoiding her concern. Ugh. The thought of anyone thinking I had a problem made me super uncomfortable and self-conscious.

Being the gal who tried to live up to an image of having it all together, I often denied (even to myself) the possibility of being on the verge of an eating disorder. After all, if our problems aren't named, they're easier to deny. Plus, I was the girl leading youth groups, knocking test scores out of the park, and doing volunteer projects. I couldn't afford to be seen as the girl who had a problem or who struggled with self-confidence. I didn't need that kind of label slapped next to my name. I wanted to be seen as Jordan, the good student; Jordan, the youth group leader; or Jordan, the sorority girl—*not* Jordan, the girl with the problem.

Well, the last weekend in October rolled around, exactly one year after Nana's death. With tears in my eyes, I ran the heck out of that half marathon. To be honest, it was healing for me. It felt like a way to finally let go of the grief I'd carried over the past year. It helped me see that I could move on from my recent breakup, and as I crossed the finish line, I realized that I was stronger than I thought I was.

After I finished that race, my relationship with food and exercise began to improve, but it didn't immediately bounce back to normal. While it improved enough to ease Mom's mind, it took time for me to really have a healthy perspective and develop better habits again. It took even longer to come to terms with how extreme it had become.

I don't share this as a sob story. I share it because I know that so many women and girls find themselves struggling with something similar. So, regardless of the details of my own story, this needs to be talked about.

I don't know your story. I hope you don't ever have to experience this or struggle with harmful behavior in any capacity. But if you have, or if you are right now, you're not alone, sister. You might be standing in that dressing room after a tough year and hating what you see in the mirror. Or you may have started a journey to better health with good intentions, but somehow along the way those intentions got lost in what has now started to become an obsession. This could be for any number of reasons, but if that's you, just let me say this: Please don't accept obsession or extreme restriction as your new normal. Set a limit and ask someone to hold you accountable so you don't slip into denial or unhealthy habits the way I did. There's no reason to journey alone.

Or maybe you're way past that and struggling with something more severe. Maybe you've been fighting this battle way longer than I did, feeling trapped at rock bottom and unable to get up. First, I want to say this isn't where your story ends and, I promise you, you aren't stuck forever.

I'm not claiming to understand your exact experience or the battle you've fought. I know my experience with this type of thing was somewhat situational and relatively short lived compared to many. Nevertheless, the year I put my body through such extreme measures did take a toll on me. So although our stories may be different, I don't want to let that hold me back from talking about it. I've learned that if we bring our battles to the light, we won't feel so beat up by them as we did when we were fighting them in secret.

See, although the extreme behavior slowly subsided after I finished that half marathon (I'll share more on what helped at the end of the chapter), that doesn't mean I was completely free.

During most of my college years, I still measured my worth by the number I saw on the scale each morning. If it was lower than the day before, I felt okay. If it was higher, I felt ashamed of what I saw in the mirror.

Through that experience I learned that when we allow lies to become labels (such as "thunder thighs" or "the girl with a problem"), we will look at ourselves through the lens of shame. When we see ourselves through a lens of shame, we don't see reality. We see what's wrong with us rather than who we are. We see a distorted view of what's really there.

We'll always find some sort of scale—the approval of others or something else—to measure our worth, coming back to it each morning, hoping just a little more progress will be enough.

Our insecurities and unrealistic expectations shape the person we believe we should be and lead us to hide who we really are just to prove we are worthy.

This was my story for nearly a year. I'd quietly count calories, squeeze in extra workouts, and guzzle down green tea diet pills when no one was watching. And if anyone expressed any amount of concern about the weight I'd lost, I'd smile and assure them everything was just fine until I believed it myself.

Even as it improved, I never spoke of it. In fact, because it began to improve, I found no need to talk about it. I wanted to pretend I never went to such extreme measures and forget about the whole thing. Denial became my normal. It became the door I hid behind. That is, until one day, as Will Smith would say, "my life got flipped turned upside down."

I'll tell you the story, but I highly recommend you get comfortable and put your big-girl panties on because we're about to go real deep, real fast.

The Door I Never Opened

I want to preface this by telling you that while I'm not here to impose my faith on you, I'm also not going to hide it from you. So if this makes you uncomfortable, well, maybe that's good. Growth comes when we leave our comfort zones.

I'm not sure if you believe in God or follow Jesus. Quite honestly, up until this particular point in my life, I'm not sure I did either. I mean, I grew up going to church and did a lot of things like youth groups and Bible studies, but there was still some part of it that just didn't feel real to me. Maybe you know what I'm talking about. People in church seemed so unapproachable and uptight.

In fact, church just felt like this thing to keep me on the straight and narrow, like a tradition I needed to get on board with rather than a real, active, and living thing in my life. In my head I associated Jesus with church pews, ankle skirts, and judgmental glares from my eleventh grade religion teacher.

By the time I got to college, I kept going to church and following the rules because of two things: fear and guilt. I wanted to have genuine faith, and while I did believe God was real, it wasn't personal yet. But my whole perspective on faith and vulnerability transformed on a cold December day when I naively planned to make a difference in someone else's life. Instead, I was the one forever changed.

I had volunteered for a community service project, delivering holiday care packages to those in local neighborhoods. I knocked on a door, a box in my hand, grinning my happiest grin.

The door opened slightly, and a young woman about my age poked her head around it, looking at me with empty eyes. Her hair was disheveled, and she wore black basketball shorts and a dirty yellow sweater; the half I could see was covered with stains. Her white-knuckle grip on the knob told me she didn't plan to let me or the other volunteers come inside—or want us to see what hid in the darkness behind her.

I held out the holiday care package, expecting her to reach out and take hold of it. To my surprise, she shook her head and began to back away into the dark room, slowly closing the door. I put out my hand to keep the door from shutting, reassuring her what I was offering her was completely free. I introduced my friends, and we explained we were serving the local community by providing free holiday care packages—filled to the brim with warm socks, toiletries, and nonperishables.

Surely she'd understand now. But she shook her head again, and I saw fear in her eyes.

I heard the voice of a child behind her, saying, "It's free! You just have to take it!"

"It's free! You just have to take it!" Such a simple but difficult step for her—and perhaps for all of us.

"No, no, no," she said firmly as she closed the door.

What the heck?

Confused, I made my way down the porch steps and toward the street with my companions, trying to understand the encounter.

Why is she so afraid? Why is she so determined to stay hidden behind that door?

I'm still not sure why she refused our gift, but I'd be willing to bet an element of embarrassment or shame was involved. Perhaps she said no because to say yes, she'd have to release her grip on the door and step out of the place where she'd been hiding and onto the porch, where every stain on her dirty yellow sweater would be exposed.

My confusion turned to sympathy as I began to think, *I feel you, girl. I don't want my mess exposed either.*

When we feel ashamed or unworthy, we hide and deny, which leads to internal isolation. And that is always dangerous.

That night the woman in the yellow sweater came to my mind again. As I thought about the encounter earlier that afternoon, I suddenly saw myself in her—the way she hid behind the door, the way she shrank back instead of stepping out. Then, I'm not kidding you, I literally felt my entire body become instantly overwhelmed by a warmth I can hardly put into words. Although it wasn't an audible voice, a message so loud and clear came through my heart and mind. It said, *The way she's living on the outside is the way you've been living on the inside.*

I about fell out of my seat.

There was just something in me that knew that was God blowing the doors off my heart, showing me I'd opened the door of my heart just far enough to peek out but never quite wide enough to be free of the image I'd built for myself. He was daring me to release my white-knuckle grip on the doorknob to the dark place where I'd been hiding.

By the time I met the girl in the yellow sweater, I had drastically backed off from extensive dieting and exercising. But on that cold December day, I suddenly saw I'd been hiding, and for the first time I knew that if you're hiding anything, you're not free.

You can't be 99 percent free and call that freedom. You can't hold on to even 1 percent of the past and say your chains are broken. Freedom must be complete in order to be called freedom.

This reality changed everything for me: the God who made the cosmos is the same God who saw my shame but called me by name, inviting me to swing the door open wide enough to walk through. He didn't see me as a set of labels. He didn't see me by my church attendance or things I could prove. He saw me through a lens of love—and love breaks through the barriers we build.

It was as if for the first time, the gospel I'd heard my whole life became personal. Everything changes when you grasp it. Here's the deal, sister: you and I both know no one is perfect. No matter how well we try to spot clean those stains on our souls with good works and religiosity, we'll never be good enough on our own. But that's what I had been trying to do for years until that day on a stranger's front porch, when God showed me that I was completely missing the point. Freedom isn't found by maintaining an image or checking religious boxes. It comes when I let my guard down and yield myself to the God who is above all (including me). It comes when I sacrifice my pride and need to prove, knowing Jesus lived the perfect life and left nothing for me to prove. That means I can either surrender or keep struggling along, trying to go at life on my own. Freedom, faith, and salvation are gifts to receive, not trophies to earn. There's nothing I can do to earn or pay for them. Same goes for you, friend. It's just like the care package I was offering the girl in the yellow sweater—*they're free; we just have to take them.* We just have to have the courage to open up and lay down our big fat egos. We need to remove ourselves as the god of our own lives and put God in that rightful place, which would require that we put ourselves below Him, right?

I love how Dr. Jordan Peterson says, "You should be on your knees to something that you actually admire. And if you don't feel like being on your knees in front of it, then perhaps you don't actually admire it, and then that means you haven't got the stage set properly."[2] (The word *admire* could be exchanged for the word *worship* here.)

This choice or posture does not eliminate personal responsibility. In fact, it requires it. This isn't just getting something handed to you on a silver platter. Instead, it is a matter of personal choice, admitting where you fall short and reaching out for help. Humility and vulnerability are necessary for faith and freedom.

Vulnerability Matters

Around that time I met my friend Mel. She has long, wavy blond hair and a fun sense of humor that almost immediately had me cracking up.

In one of our first conversations, we laughed so hard we almost peed our pants and got shushed multiple times during a sorority chapter meeting.

I invited her to dinner later that week so we could talk more. I just knew we'd be great friends. As we sat at a tiny table in a restaurant on Kirkwood Avenue, the main street in our beloved little college town, we swapped stories, laughed over pizza, shared our postgraduation dreams—and stayed until closing.

That's when you know a conversation is good—when you laugh so hard tears make their way down your cheeks and you manage to close the place down without even realizing how much time has passed.

That night in a pizza pub was just the beginning of one of my most treasured friendships, and it led to long road trips to small southern towns and spontaneous movie nights with more laugh-till-you-cry and cry-till-you-laugh kind of moments.

One day, as we were driving through town, she blurted out, "Can I be honest about something?"

Fighting back tears, Mel shared from her heart about some decisions she wished she hadn't made, and in a near whisper she admitted to struggling with extreme dieting and a really toxic relationship with food and her weight.

Words came out of my mouth faster than I could hold them back. It's as if my heart leaped out of my chest and laid itself on the dashboard before I could think twice about it.

There I was, baring my soul, feeling totally stripped down and vulnerable yet somehow more alive than I had felt in a while.

Honesty paved the way for a deeper discussion, and we both found redeeming freedom and purpose in that. Mel listened intently as I told her about how God used the encounter with the woman in the yellow sweater to meet me and how experiencing His love in such a personal way was a huge step in setting me free from the lies I had believed about myself for years.

Tears welled in Mel's eyes, and just like that, doors turned into doorways, and walls between us turned into hallways connecting our hearts.

Vulnerability is the key to overcoming the trap that shame sets. That doesn't mean we have to share our stories with *everybody*. We can be wise and intentional about how we share our stories, but, gal, I'm telling you, this is a big deal.

Shame will try to hold you in the dark places because vulnerably exposing the not-so-pretty parts of your story is scary. However, the not-so-pretty parts are often the most powerful.

What do you need to open up about? What shame have you been carrying, whether it's from a mistake you made, something that happened to you, or a lie you believe about yourself? Tell a parent, friend, mentor, or counselor what has been holding you in shame and ask for help to break its grip.

I'm telling you, vulnerability—confession—is healing.[3] The stains on our hearts—the shame from flaws, mistakes, or experiences we've allowed to become a part of our identity—are removed when we refuse to be held back and bravely expose them to the light.

Over the years I've watched Mel set down her shame and share her story, boldly inviting those living in the deepest shame to walk in the same freedom. When we open our doors just a little wider, we give someone else permission to do the same.

It dawned on me that *friendship is a lifeline for living with purpose.* You can't live your purpose without that kind of love. Love is the lifeline.

Sister, if you struggle with shame, let me tell you that you're not alone and that only you get to decide if it has the power to hold you back from receiving the freedom and living the life God wants for you.

You want to make an impact in this world? You want to get unstuck and outside yourself? Please don't be stubborn like I was. Please don't refuse to ask for help or live in denial because you somehow think that makes you stronger. Take the pressure off yourself to be somebody and open your door to the some-bodies in front of you.

We don't break through shame by hiding behind a reputation or by living under the pressure to measure up to the expectations we perceive others have of us. We break through it by bravely surrendering our pride and opening our doors, one confession and one conversation at a time. And, yeah, it can be really uncomfortable. But I wholeheartedly believe that God didn't wreck me on that cold December day for no reason. He didn't give me a story just to hide it in shame. He gave me a story because it needs to be *shared*—even when I'm afraid that others will think it's lame. The same is true for you.

I speak from personal experience when I say that *vulnerability works—and it matters*. I dare you—no, I *beg* you—to open up, to ask for help, and to share where you *really* are. As Dr. Brené Brown said in her book *Rising Strong,* "Vulnerability is not weakness; it's our greatest measure of courage."[4]

Who is one person on your heart you can reach out to and share with? Take an intentional step and invite that person to lunch. You don't have to have it all figured out. You won't have an answer to every question. But you *can* open up, share, and hug—and that's always enough to start with.

Know why? Because your story won't just change you; when you share it, it has the power to change someone else. And I think that alone is worth it.

P.S. Read Me

I want to take a quick second to share with you a few practical steps that helped me, in case you struggle with something like I did.

As I said, the ultimate thing that helped me completely

overcome my unhealthy and obsessive behavior with food and exercise was opening my heart to the love of God in a personal way. I truly believe that He alone has the power to heal all wounds.

However, there were also a few other tangible steps that helped me maintain continued growth. Keep in mind that the following suggestions are not meant to replace professional help, but since they helped me (and friends of mine), I believe they are worth sharing with you.

1. Find a Healthy Community

As I became aware of the types of environments and relationships that made my behavior and choices more extreme (such as social circles that focused on image and status), I focused on building more intentional and deeper friendships with like-minded people who truly wanted the best for me.

Thankfully, I was blessed to find a healthy community of people who really sharpened and uplifted me. Developing these relationships took longer than just becoming friends with the first person who was nice to me, but this investment proved to be life changing in the end.

Look at your circle. Do you feel you have to change how you look to fit in? Is it a life-giving situation or a constant comparison game, full of drama and one-upping one another?

They say you begin to look like the five people you spend

the most time with. Who are your top five? Do you need to change who they are?

2. Identify Your Triggers and Eliminate Them

For me, the scale and calories were the triggers. If I stepped on a scale and didn't like what I saw, I'd force myself to work out extra hard and not eat anything that day until the number on the scale was back to what I wanted. Or if I saw a menu item that was full of healthy fats, good protein, and other nutrients but it had more than a certain number of calories, I'd order a small salad instead, just to avoid going over that *one* number limit (even though I was also limiting my numbers when it came to other good things like protein).

In my recovery from this obsession, I made incremental adjustments that helped create sustainable change. I don't remember all the specifics anymore, but I will give you an example of what helped me.

Since the scale and calories were my triggers, I made small adjustments to these two things. For example, I decreased the number of times I checked my weight each week (from every day to just a couple of times per week) and increased my calorie intake a little bit at a time. In other words, I didn't just delete my calorie counter app as if it was no big deal. I simply made an adjustment, slowly bumping up my daily intake limit to a healthier number. Doing this helped me make the mental shift that a bit more food was okay—because my tracker showed me it was.

Then, after some time, I resolved to weigh myself only once per week and bumped the intake a bit more again, which helped me get a little closer to what was actually sustainable. A few months of making these small adjustments to my extreme behaviors helped slowly shift my entire mind-set and therefore habits. This led to slowly regaining control.

If you've struggled with disordered eating, extreme dieting and exercise, binge eating, or any other unhealthy habit, I dare you to call it out, write down what needs to change, and commit to making one change at a time, one week or month at a time. Ask someone to hold you accountable, and track your progress so you don't lose motivation. This makes a big difference.

3. Set Goals and Boundaries

I feel as though everywhere I look, I see motivational speakers and fitness accounts on social media telling us to go after our health and fitness goals.

Whenever I see them, one half of me claps and says, "Yes, sister! Preach it!" but the other half thinks something critical might be missing.

That critical something is health and fitness *boundaries*. If we are going to lead purposeful lives, we must have enough discipline not to lead *obsessive* lives. However, I know from personal experience that when we talk only about the goals we're going after in this area, it's easy to get tunnel vision and stop seeing the full picture.

When my behavior became really extreme leading up to that half marathon, I had convinced myself I was just working toward a big goal. Since I didn't put any kind of boundaries on that goal, it essentially took over my life.

Girl, please remain committed to your goals, but please do not become so obsessed with them that you forget there is more to your worth than whether you hit that number or go to the gym five days a week.

I'm not suggesting you drop all your goals, especially if they are healthy or recommended by a doctor. In fact, I'd be the first to cheer you on as you take initiative to achieve them. However, I am suggesting you set up some boundaries to keep your mind in the right place.

When I began to set sensible goals and coupled those with boundaries (such as the pace at which I worked toward them), I experienced so much more balance. That also meant I was less inclined toward obsessive behavior in my life.

Keep this simple. If your goal is to work out five days per week, set a boundary to go alongside it. That boundary might be that you don't work out more than thirty minutes each day or that you don't track calories consumed so that numbers do not become an obsession for you. If you're on a journey to gain or lose ten pounds, set a boundary by seeking accountability so that eating well doesn't turn into overeating or not eating enough.

Consistently opening up about where you are and where you're headed will keep you on track with your goals while simultaneously allowing you to remain unashamed.

4. Don't Let Shame Stop You from Getting Help

I didn't seek help, but I really should have. Technically, Mom did seek out some medical help on my behalf, even though I didn't see the need. However, friends of mine who have struggled with this were smart enough to seek out professional help, and it was game changing for them.

Sis, your body is a temple, not a trophy. And only *you* get to decide what lens you'll look through. To be truly free of an unhealthy mind-set and harmful behaviors, you have to look at fitness and health as part of your self-care, not part of your self-worth—and there is no shame in reaching out and asking for assistance to get there.

Choose wisely. Open up and ask for help. You were not made to be a one-woman show.

7

Overcoming Comparison with Compassion and Communication

You know that feeling that comes when you see all your friends posting their cool new opportunities or milestones on social media and then you look at what you're doing (or not doing) with your life and wish it was way cooler than it is? Or when you find yourself wishing you had more friends in your new city? When these things happen, that little voice in your head shouts, *I have got to figure out my life!*

That, my friend, is called comparison-induced pressure. Yes, I totally made that up, and I'm not a psychologist, so that may not be at all what it's technically called. That's what I call it though.

If you're struggling with it, welcome to the club. I felt like that so much during my first year out of college because all my friends had legit jobs, and I was wearing about five different hats, from part-time blogger to part-time wedding venue contract worker to photography business owner (that phase lasted less than a year) to newlywed wife. All fun and good things. But try juggling them all at once while everyone else seems to have it figured out. *Hello, major insecurity.*

Comparison is the pits, man. Seriously. Especially in those awkward postgrad years, or any season of transition, really.

I'm sure we all know what comparison feels like, and you and I can probably both identify it in ourselves. However, I think we sometimes stop there. We agree that it's unhealthy without actually breaking down the effects it has on us or taking action steps to grow beyond it.

Unfortunately, comparison can be so stinking easy to expend a lot of valuable energy on, become distracted by, *and* get stuck in.

I remember one time a few years ago, I had an experience that gave me a really clear picture of what I was actually doing every time I allowed room for comparison. Come with me to the gym where I used to train, and I'll give you a peek into what happened.

It was a late afternoon like any other. I filled my water bottle and laced up my favorite sneakers before heading to the gym. When I walked into the fitness center, I saw a disheartening sight: only one treadmill was available.

One. And I didn't want to use that one. I paced back and forth across the back of the room for a time, disguising my stalling with stretching and warm-ups, secretly hoping someone else would claim the last treadmill. Call me crazy, but I really don't like running on a machine with people on both my right and left. I worry that they can hear me panting or that my sweat will fly into my neighbor's face, and I feel claustrophobic. It's awkward. (Am I the only one?)

But this time there didn't seem to be any way out of it.

Five long minutes passed. No one in the entire gym seemed ready to abandon his treadmill, nor did anyone want the available treadmill. I made my way there, slowly, all the while hoping someone else would beat me to it. Of course, no one did. Begrudgingly, I stepped up and joined the long line of synchronized joggers.

An older gentleman was power walking to my left. *I had better go faster than him.*

To my right was a young woman dressed in a coordinating athletic outfit. She wore her hair in a neat ponytail, and her voluminous curls swished with each stride. She had long, powerful legs, and she sprinted effortlessly.

And there I was in my five-dollar gray Walmart sweatshirt, old gym shorts with paint stains, and Christmas penguin socks peeking out over my shoes. (They were the only clean pair left; don't judge me.) I glanced over to check out her speed: 6.9 miles an hour! *I can do that. I have to keep up with her.* I set my speed to 7.0 miles an hour and took off, practically sprinting in place.

And so it began—the competition, I mean. Not a real competition, of course. It was all in my mind. She had no idea she and I were battling for first place, and no one but me was keeping score. No one was getting a trophy. But I *had* to keep up with her, and you'd better believe I had to at least outrun the guy on my left.

We do that, don't we? Gauge how we measure up to the people around us—whether we're ahead or behind, better or worse? Though it might seem to challenge or even push us onward, this tendency limits what we could achieve if we stopped comparing ourselves with others and started running our own race.

Comparison Doesn't Take You Anywhere

As I was panting on the treadmill, running a race that didn't actually exist, it all clicked in my brain: giving in to comparison is kind of like running on a treadmill. It's exhausting but doesn't really take you anywhere.

My treadmill competition taught me that when I live in

comparison, I get into a tiresome cycle of hustling to keep up with and outrun others but not heading anywhere worthwhile. I mean, I was quite literally, as well as figuratively, sprinting in place in that moment.

I think we can all agree that comparison only tires us out and distracts us. That's undeniable. However, I want to get a little more specific. As I've reflected on all the ways I struggle with comparison, I've examined times in my life when comparison got the better of me, the treadmill race being only one of many. The more I examined these experiences, the more I recognized three ways comparison kept recurring:

1. I compare my looks, success, or status with that of others.
2. I compare how I measure up to my own expectations.
3. I compare my issues to other people's issues.

Let's look at each of these types of comparison so we can learn to identify and eliminate them.

1. We Compare Our Looks, Success, or Status

This is the most common type of comparison. We all know what it's like to see how well someone else is doing and have thoughts such as *Why can't I have what she has?* or *If only I had her job/friends/body/talent/life, I'd be happy.*

That day on the treadmill, I missed something I think we

all miss. I didn't fill in the gaps; I didn't consider the rest of the story. Here's what I mean: I didn't know how long either of my neighbors had been on the treadmill. I immediately assumed one was behind me and the other was ahead of me in accomplishment based on what I saw, without first considering context, which would likely have minimized the comparison distance between us. I should have asked myself these questions:

- *Why are they jogging/power walking in the first place?*
- *Are they in training?*
- *What are they working toward?*

Imagining likely scenarios could have prevented the comparison. The older man might have been trying to keep his heart healthy, and maybe the young woman was training for an upcoming race. She could have been a professional runner for all I know, or maybe her trainer had her on a rigorous training program. Maybe they both were taking steps toward wellness, or maybe they had been at it far longer than I had. The man may have been on the treadmill for fifty minutes already, the woman may have been running for only fifteen, and I was just getting started. If so, we had all started at different times and were at different places in our workouts.

I didn't know where they came from, what their stories

were, or where they were on the journey. I saw only their current performance and weighed it against my own.

When this kind of comparison creeps in, I have to remind myself of something really important: *I have to stop observing where others are if I have any hope of serving my purpose right where I am.*

Sister, I hate to bum you out, but the same is true for you. You cannot live a purposeful life if you are so preoccupied with trying to make it look like someone else's. We have got to get this through our noggins.

2. We Compare How We Measure Up to Our Own Expectations

Whether intentionally or unintentionally, most of us have expectations for what we think our lives will look like. We may have thoughts like this:

- *By the time I'm thirty-five, I'll be married with two kids.*
- *I'll advance quickly in my company.*
- *I'll work hard to keep my house spotless.*
- *If I excel, I'll get into grad school and live my dream.*

The danger in constantly comparing our everyday reality with the ideals or expectations we have comes when our real experiences don't measure up to our expectations. That can cause us to lose heart and feel hopeless, to be disillusioned and disenchanted.

While I'm a strong advocate for goal setting, I also think it's important to remember that when we fixate on what life *should* be or how things *could* look, we can lack direction in the here and now. When the story we thought would be best for us is a long way from the life we're living, we begin to compare the two, which inevitably leads to a life driven by discontentment, not intentionality.

The comparisons we make and the expectations we have can easily hinder us and weigh us down. Then we become exhausted.

Look at your own life. Have you ever experienced a massive gap between your expectations and your actual experience? Did that motivate you to live more intentionally? Or did it defeat and discourage you?

3. We Compare Our Issues

Last, we compare our issues. *Wait. We compare our issues?* Think about how absurd that sounds. But we do. We compare our struggles and our shortcomings just as much as we compare our successes and performances.

How often have you seen what someone else is going

through and immediately felt guilty for struggling with something that seems less serious? Or maybe you've gone through a tragedy and then heard someone share what she's struggling with and thought to yourself, *How dare she? She hasn't walked through half of what I have!*

An experience you deem insignificant might be the deepest kind of brokenness another person has faced in her lifetime. On the surface her struggle may not seem that hard, but it could be debilitating to her. Another person might be so familiar with severe trauma or tragedy that you assume she won't understand your simple struggle because she's walked through so much worse.

Why do we do that? I mean, since when are our struggles measured on a scale? Why do we try to compare our joy *and* our junk? What purpose does that serve other than feeding bitterness? Where does that take us? We spend a lot of our energy assuming and categorizing instead of empathizing and connecting. And it needs to stop.

When we compare our stories and rank our struggles using some imaginary tier system that was never meant to exist, we hurt only ourselves. We might walk through different types of brokenness; we might experience different struggles or carry different pain. But discrediting someone else's experiences in comparison with our own—or vice versa—is unfruitful, divisive, and unproductive. The real challenge is to learn to have compassion for both ourselves and for the people next to us, even when it seems as if they're better off than we are.

Adjustment Strategies That Help Me Quit Comparing

I don't know about you, but I have a hard time believing women can just stop comparing themselves to others, as if they're superhuman. Is there a switch you can just flip on and off that I'm unaware of?

While I do believe it's possible to drastically cut down on how much we compare ourselves to others, I think it's helpful to have actual steps to follow.

Maybe you haven't noticed, but I'm a practical kind of gal. I could *tell* you all day long to stop comparing yourself, sure. But I'd rather give you some practical ideas for how to overcome comparison. I often have to ask myself, *What steps can I take today to replace the energy I'm wasting on comparison and reinvest that energy into compassion, connection, and creating community?*

Here are a few ways I've seen this work most effectively in my own life:

1. Remember your "why."
2. Replace jealous thoughts with joyful thoughts.

3. Practice gratitude and cheerful generosity.

4. Let her win.

5. Communicate.

Lean in. Let's look at each one of these.

1. Remember Your "Why"

Perhaps one of the simplest ways I combat comparison is by actively replacing the energy wasted on comparison with energy that focuses on accomplishing the task I originally set out to achieve.

For example, if I find I'm comparing myself to a neighboring runner on the treadmill, I can nip that in the bud quickly by asking myself, *Why am I on this treadmill to begin with? What is my "why"? Did I come here to race or to steward my health?*

When I take a moment to reframe my thoughts and remember my "why," it helps me focus on what I came to do.

This is an incredibly simple discipline that can make all the difference. If you begin to notice you compare your business to a friend's, remember your "why" by asking yourself this question: *Why did I start my business? Did I start it to feed my family and make a difference, or did I start it to outdo my friend?*

Or if you compare yourself with others on social media, consider your "why" for using that space: *Why do I use this? What is the purpose of it? Am I using it as a tool to encourage, influence, or market to a specific audience? Or am I using it to keep up with strangers on the internet?*

If you're not sure what your purpose for doing something is, you'll do it aimlessly and unintentionally. On the flip side, if you have a deeper why to guide every little thing you do and actively use it to combat comparison (and other distractions), you'll find you are not only more fulfilled by what you're doing but also more focused on what matters most. Keep the purpose behind whatever you're doing in mind, and use that to help you focus on owning *your* everyday, not theirs.

2. Replace Jealous Thoughts with Joyful Thoughts

I constantly compared myself with a certain girl on the playground in fifth grade. Let's call her Liz. Liz was my archenemy because the boy I had a megacrush on had a megacrush on her. She had long dark hair and porcelain skin. I'd look out from the top of the jungle gym, my very own watchtower, only to see my crush make googly eyes over her as she jumped rope, her perfect hair bouncing with each pretty little jump she made. If the heart-eye emoji existed back then, that would have been his face. *Puke.*

One day he let her borrow his sweatshirt. There she was, frolicking about in his Axe-drenched sweatshirt during recess. And there I was with a ketchup stain down the front of my T-shirt, watching her from afar, oozing jealousy.

At the time, I didn't know half of what Liz was going through in her personal life. I didn't know a thing about how kind she was or how much I might like her if I got to know her. I just knew she'd beaten me in the boy department, and therefore I didn't like her.

This is a silly childhood memory, but it accurately illustrates what so many of us feel even in our adult lives as we observe others on a screen or from the next cubicle over—our own grown-up watchtowers.

It's hard to be joyful when I allow someone else's happiness to make me miserable. However, my misery is not the problem; it is a *symptom* of the problem. The real problem is my thought life. I have to remember that I *do* have some power over which thoughts I allow to stay and which thoughts I remove and replace.¹ And so do you.

Jealous thoughts create comparison, which leads to division, misunderstanding, and isolation. On the other hand, when we take a step back, those jealous thoughts not only fade but can even be replaced with joyful thoughts. As I've grown older, I've had to develop the discipline of replacing jealous thoughts with truths that bring me joy. If I find myself thinking a toxic thought about someone I'm watching from afar, I commit to matching that jealous thought with *two* healthy thoughts.

For example, if I think to myself, *I dislike that she is just so much more _____ than I am,* then I must match that thought with statements or affirmations like these:

- I will love who I am right now because where I am is exactly where I'm meant to be.
- As I change my thoughts, my heart posture changes.
- Her success is not my failure.
- I am fully known and fully loved at my worst, not just at my best.
- What is happening to me today is the very best thing for me now and for who I will become tomorrow.

Who is your Liz, the one you watch from afar with unwarranted disdain? Do you have her in mind? Are those jealous thoughts creeping up? If so, write down two joyful thoughts to replace (and outnumber) them. They can be about her, or they can be two thoughts that affirm what you know to be true and that allow you to see life through a lens of love and gratitude.

3. Practice Gratitude and Cheerful Generosity

When I compare myself with others or compare my expectations with my reality and feel that I somehow come up short, I often begin to complain. Complaining, or grumbling, is usually the by-product of comparison.

You and I cannot do what we're made to do, fulfill our

purpose, or be lights in this generation if we're tripped up by grumbling and complaining.[6]

One simple, tangible way to compare less is to take note of when you begin to grumble and to replace that negative energy with gratitude. When I live from a place of gratitude, I tend to be more generous than I am jealous. The more I give with a compassionate heart, the less I hold on to my expectations or earthly desires that drive me to compare.

I know my natural tendency is to cling tightly to my resources, expectations, finances, and more. But I also know how much depending on my things can make me focus on what I lack rather than on how I can love. That said, when I focus on gratitude, I experience more freedom and willingness to give. Giving blesses not just others but also me because the looser the grip I have on my things, the less these things will have a grip on me.

One thing you can do today is write down everything you are grateful for on sticky notes and put them all over your house where you will see them. You could also write this list as a note on your phone and set it as your wallpaper. Every time you notice yourself grumbling, revisit and read through your gratitude list.

Then discern how you might be able to give a little of what you are grateful for to someone else. Get up and do it immediately. Don't hesitate, or you'll never actually do it. The more you are grateful for and give away what you have, the less you'll grumble about what you don't have.

4. Let Her Win

Let's go back to my treadmill competition, where I found myself secretly competing against my neighboring runner. For several minutes I was able to keep up. I was even able to go a little faster for a few seconds. I'd catch myself leaning over to see her speed, wanting to make sure that she was still at least a few steps behind me—that I was winning. (I feel so weird admitting this.) It's ridiculous, I know, but that's what comparison is: ridiculous.

Then my little imaginary competition blew up. I looked over to see that she had increased her speed and was comfortably running much faster. She'd won.

How in the world?

For half a second I was frustrated, but then I felt relief—even freedom. It was as if I had become distracted by a fake competition, focused on how I was outdoing her and how I could stay ahead. When she won, the competition was over, and oddly, I was okay with it. I didn't have to keep trying to outrun her for no reason other than outrunning her. That's an exhausting way to live.

It's not as if my own workout suffered when she bypassed

me either. Rather than taking anything away from what I was doing, her winning helped me refocus on what I came to do in the first place.

You may not compete this way, but you might compete in other ways. Think about those with whom you're most likely to create competitions in your own mind—at your workplace, in your community, or elsewhere. Now ask yourself, *Have I become distracted by the illusion of staying one step ahead?*

How can you break through it? Let her win the competition you've created in your mind. It is so freeing to take yourself out of a competition that doesn't actually exist.

It is truly that simple. Perhaps the best way to put this into action is to practice cheering others on. Practical ways to do this include encouraging the one you envy or even promoting or supporting the work of someone with whom you'd otherwise compete. As an author, I try to share books by other authors, especially those in my niche. By championing them, I chip away at the temptation to compete with them. Helping them win, instead of trying to beat them, allows me to connect with them. Instead of running against others, I get the freedom and fun of running *with* them.

While a little competition can be healthy, it's important to evaluate what we're really focused on and how it might actually be tripping us up more than spurring us on.

Think of someone you envy or compare yourself to. Reach out and encourage that person. Who does the world say is a competitor in your industry or work? Consider what you can do to come alongside that individual instead.

5. Communicate

A few months ago, my husband and I decided to be a little ambitious and start a new routine that required getting up at 5:00 a.m. to work out. We signed up for a monthly gym membership and got to work. I'll be honest, I gave myself major kudos for getting my booty on a treadmill before the sun came up. A few days in, I noticed there was another gal who also had some major ambition, and she wasn't just walking on the treadmill. She was doing intense HIIT (high-intensity interval training) workouts, with barely any breaks, day after day after day. Even my husband pointed it out, and we both were shocked at her level of effort, especially without a trainer!

Okay, I know, I have an issue of comparing myself to other women at the gym. However, I'm admitting it because I'd be willing to bet at least a couple of bucks you've done the same in an environment where you spend a lot of time, whether that's at the gym, at the office, online, or somewhere else.

Anyway, at the time, I refused to do anything with weights at the gym because I didn't know much about proper form, so

I felt super awkward any time I tried. Of course, this lady's form looked flawless, so I continued to avoid the weights and stayed in my comfort zone on the treadmill.

A few weeks into our early-morning workout routine, I had to walk past her section to get a mat, and we made eye contact. She smiled at me as if to say hello.

Oh, shoot, now I have to say something!

Thinking on my toes (which is quite the feat at 5:30 a.m.), I said, "Hey, what kind of workout are you doing? Is it HIIT?"

To my surprise, she responded, "Yeah! You should do it with me sometime!"

I about died. I did *not* want to go through one of her Navy Seal–level workouts, but I was not about to say no and look like a weenie.

Of course I responded, "Sure! How's Wednesday?"

"Wednesday's perfect! Meet me here at 5:30!"

So at that point I had a workout date with a woman whose name I didn't even know.

I was not about to skip it, though. I was not about to go back to the gym every day and wonder if she thought I was a chicken for backing out.

No way.

On Wednesday morning I rolled up to the gym, said a little prayer, and walked in to see her stretching and warming up.

Turns out I didn't die. I survived the workout. It wasn't as bad as I thought it would be. In fact, it was good to be pushed outside my comfort zone.

And guess what? I actually really liked her. Before I connected with her personally, I made up this whole ridiculous story about her in my mind based on her form and motivation level in the gym. I assumed if she was that ambitious in the gym every day, she must also have an insanely high-paying job and a private jet and meetings with the president or something. Turns out none of that is true. She's a normal woman like me. She just goes to bed early and has lots of energy in the morning. Go figure.

As we talked about shared interests, our dreams, and more, she asked what I did for work. I happened to mention I would be speaking at a local event the next day, and she asked if she could come support me!

This lady had spent a grand total of one hour with me (when I was sweating and half-awake) and was already asking to come cheer me on. She didn't just offer either. She actually came to the event the next day.

It blew my socks off.

Know what this taught me? It taught me that the people we judge, envy, or compare ourselves to most are sometimes the people we might like most if we actually sat down and got to know them.

The fact of the matter is this: either I can compare myself to others from afar, or I can get a little closer and communicate. Instead of assuming they're just doing ten times better at life than I am, I can ask a question and get to know them a little more.

The same is true for you, sister. Ask more than you assume, and communicate more than you compare. This is a simple way to purposefully break through petty concerns and the pressure to prove. Try it next time. It might just change your life.

8

Overcoming Perfectionism by Prioritizing

Every summer my girlfriends and I spend many slow small-town evenings together. The sidesplitting laughter and memories we share around bonfires and kitchen tables are my absolute favorite. We savor these ordinary Indiana evenings for what they are: real and simple. We all show up just as we are—with hungry bellies and wearing comfy T-shirts. There's no exquisite menu or dinner reservation; we just search through pantries and raid refrigerators for whatever we can find. Perfection isn't required.

Perhaps what makes these nights so special is that we're all in such different seasons of life—from singleness to newly married to motherhood—and as a result we bring a refreshing variety of perspectives to any good conversation. Connection happens on a deeper level and dares us to look deep into our souls. These evenings are also my favorite because even when we're doing nothing spectacular, the most spectacular things happen.

One of our recent conversations started like any other, but it stands out in my memory because it challenged me in the very best way. As we sat at Hannah's kitchen counter, the summer sun was just beginning to set over the cornfields, casting a golden light through the kitchen windows. Hannah stood across from me, making guacamole and telling me about her special recipe as she added a little garlic. Hank, her old pug, snored contentedly in the corner. Our friend Lindsey, wearing comfortable blue sweatpants and a fitted tee that stretched ever so slightly over her baby bump, sliced apples.

As we chatted over popcorn, chips, guacamole, and apple slices, Lindsey raised a question. "In what area are you most likely to be a perfectionist?"

Hannah and I looked at her, neither of us wanting to answer first. An awkward silence filled the room, broken only by Hank's snoring.

Um, everything, I thought to myself.

I finally spoke up as I reached for the popcorn. "I tend to put pressure on myself to do everything right and be a perfect example. No one forced it on me; I just kind of put that pressure on myself. My unrealistic expectations for myself have affected my marriage, my work, and even my confidence. I often feel as though I must either be the best at something or not try it at all. And other times I feel pressure to do it all, like I have to be everything to everyone or I'm just a letdown."

Lindsey nodded her head in understanding, reached over, and squeezed my shoulder.

Hannah chimed in, sharing that she's held her body to a standard of perfection, even to the point of self-loathing and harmful behavior. "I don't like certain things about my body, and I sometimes care far too much about what others think."

"What about you, Linds?" she asked as she crunched on an apple slice.

"I totally relate to the body image struggle, since I was a child model and an NFL cheerleader," she said. "By God's grace I've found so much freedom from that, but in this season of life, I've been such a perfectionist about my home. It really bothers me when my house isn't clean. I know I have a toddler at home and a baby on the way, but it's as if I'm afraid people will think I'm not responsible if my home isn't spotless or well decorated. I'm also a perfectionist about my parenting—but that's a whole other conversation," she said with a chuckle.

All tension breaks in moments like that.

It's as if you know somewhere deep inside that you're not the only one, but when someone else is brave enough to actually say it, you suddenly feel way less alone.

We talked for hours, sharing what we're really like—how prideful we are and how self-righteous we can be. The conversation went even deeper as we shared how, at times, we've turned our marriages, families, faith, and relationships into to-do lists and performances to obtain a picture-perfect result instead of pursuing purpose.

I want to invite you to the kitchen table and into this conversation as the sun sets over the cornfields and streams through the windows. Have some popcorn. Or try some guacamole. This is a grace place. A seat at the table is ready for you. Come inside and spill: In what areas of life are *you* a perfectionist? In your career? Your grades? Your appearance? Your plans? Your marriage or family? Your home?

The answer isn't to stop caring about those things, and it certainly doesn't help to be told, "Well, just stop being such a perfectionist!" What helps me is getting to the *root* of the issue. When you think of the ways you tend to be a perfectionist, it's important to consider the reason. For example, if you're a perfectionist in a relationship, is it because you're struggling with insecurity? Do you fear the relationship could crumble? Or do you worry what others will think about your relationship? If you're a perfectionist about your grades in school or your performance at work, is it because you fear failure? Do you put your identity in what you can achieve? If you're a people pleaser, is it because you hate disappointing people? Or because you crave the praise of others?

Whatever it is, here's what I've learned in my own life: the root of my perfectionism is insecurity. I'd bet the same is true for you. If you go deeper, where do you think that insecurity, fear, and worry ultimately come from? What are you afraid of? Let me guess. Not being loved. Not being accepted. Not being wanted, seen, affirmed, or praised. *Not having a noteworthy purpose.*

What causes us to desperately crave approval, affirmation, and applause? Pride. Pride warps our view of God and is sneaky about making us into our own god. We end up serving ourselves—even when it looks as if we're serving others— because of pride.

Three Ways Perfectionism Holds Me Back

After that long kitchen conversation, I was curious to learn more about perfectionism, just to gain a better understanding of it. One of the definitions of *perfectionism* in *Merriam-Webster* is "the setting of unrealistically demanding goals accompanied by a disposition to regard failure to achieve them as unacceptable and a sign of personal worthlessness."[7] When I did some research, I found something interesting:

> What makes perfectionism so toxic is that while those in its grip desire success, *they are most focused on avoiding failure,* so theirs is a negative orientation. And love isn't a refuge; in fact, it feels way too conditional on performance.[8]

Let's unpack this a bit.

1. *Love Feels Conditional on Performance*

For those caught up in perfectionism (guilty here), love is not a refuge, because it feels conditional, as if receiving love depends on our performance. Do you see that? That's the ultimate problem for perfectionists—love is something we earn when we perform well.

More than that, perfectionism distorts our ability to love because it warps our understanding of love. When we operate out of perfectionism rather than purpose, we don't fully allow ourselves to receive love—only to earn it.

When I'm driven by perfectionism or living into perceived expectations, I essentially prioritize performance over purpose and fail to do what I'm ultimately made to do—love God, love people, and let myself be loved. If I don't truly believe I am loved, I can't give away something I don't have.

2. Perfectionism Makes Me the Focus

Imagine living in a house where mirrors have replaced all the windows. It would be dark inside, and the only thing you would see is yourself. You wouldn't be able to see sunshine or what was going on in the world outside. That's kind of what living in perfectionism is like. Perfectionism and pride rob me of purpose because all I see is myself. As my friends and I sat around the table, I came to a conclusion: as women of purpose, we need to spend less time looking at our reflection in the mirror and more time reflecting light and love to the world.

Perfectionism says, "Look at me. I've got it all together!" Purpose says, "Hey, sister, let's do this together."

A differentiating factor between perfectionism and purpose is this: perfectionism boxes us into ourselves, but purpose calls us outside ourselves—outside our imperfections and obsessions and into the lives of others.

Perfectionism drives us to cover up every flaw and to project spotless images of ourselves, our accomplishments, and our worthiness. But living our purpose doesn't make us the point; it makes us point to the One who is the point. (How's that for a tongue twister?)

What do *you* see when you look in the mirror? Do you see a woman beaten down by perfectionism or a woman who reflects God's love and is propelled by her purpose?

3. Priorities Are Replaced by the Fear of Failure

As I told my girlfriends, I never want to fail anyone. I don't want to fail as a wife. I don't want to fail as a friend. I don't want to fail as a leader in my work and community. I don't want to fail as a daughter, neighbor, or volunteer. The list could go on, but I'm sure you get the point.

I don't want to fail at anything or let anyone down.

Since perfectionism isn't so much about succeeding as it is about avoiding failure, it makes sense that we feel we need to do it all and that we even fall into people pleasing just to prove to ourselves (and likely to others) that we're enough. The desire to avoid failure, however, can quickly cause suffocating pressure to be everything to everybody and to do it all. We take on things that only weigh us down, and inevitably, the pressure increases.

I've found that when I operate under the fear of failure, I'm weighed down by the pressure to prove myself and I lose sight of the one priority that matters: what God has given me to do in this season of life.

Do you feel this pressure too and cave in to the demands of your perceived expectations? Have you said things like this to yourself:

- *I don't want to fail my friend.*
- *I don't want to let anyone down, so I'll commit to this extra activity even though I know it'll be tough to squeeze in.*
- *I don't want to come up short as the team captain, classroom mom, or _____.*

Dear one, hear me. In pursuit of your purpose, you will disappoint or let others down from time to time. Don't let that discourage you. Don't let it defeat you. You can't do your best at what God designed you to do if you're distracted with running about, trying to be everything to everyone. It just doesn't work like that.

Preach that to yourself. Over and over until it sticks in your brain. Seriously.

You can't do *all* things well; you can't give your best in a few things if you're striving to be the best in all things. You can try, sure, but you'll reach the limit of human capacity. You'll begin to cut corners or snap at your loved ones because the pressure is too much. Your heart will get weary. You won't be able to give your best because you'll be so distracted just trying to be the best. You'll miss divine appointments because all your other appointments are endless and your to-do list is too long. (I'm preaching to myself here.)

I love the quote that says, "I am a human being, not a human doing."[9] Purpose is found not in trying to prove we're worthy but in prioritizing what's important so we can be more present in being who we are made to be.

I think in our efforts to avoid failure in all things, we mistakenly fail to be faithful in the small things that truly matter. We must relentlessly remove the pressure to prove and to please people by prioritizing what matters most.

Choose three areas you'll focus on and faithfully steward in this season, and then break those three priorities down into subpriorities. For example, if one of my core priorities is my marriage, that means I need to have three subpriorities for how I steward my marriage. Matt and I have three consistent things we prioritize within our marriage to keep it healthy: Sunday afternoons together with uninterrupted time to plan our weeks (no phones); consistent routines together (dinnertime, morning workouts, etc.); and biweekly marriage counseling meetings.

Pick your top three priorities and then allow yourself the freedom to fail at the rest. By fail, I don't mean totally neglect everything else in your life, but I do mean give yourself permission to be less available for those things that are not top priorities. Otherwise you'll begin to neglect what you say your top priorities are. Focusing on your priorities may mean that some friends won't stick around or that you'll grow apart for a season. That is okay. No one can faithfully steward dozens of deep, meaningful relationships at one time anyway. Keep in mind that it's okay to prioritize quality over quantity as we steward what matters most.

When I lose sight of this or I can't be present in what's important because my priorities are out of whack, something has to go. As my wise mother-in-law says, "Bless and release." *Release* the pressures that weigh you down so you can *receive* the fruit that comes when you steward your priorities well. Trying to operate beyond your capacity just to prove something will not only hurt you but also become a barrier that hinders you. Perhaps we must fail at some things to be faithful in the few things that matter most.

Quit Operating in Extremes

If I'm not careful, I can start to live in extremes. For example, if perfectionism drives me and my decisions for too long, I eventually hit a wall and burn out because I'll never actually reach perfection. All my effort will feel wasted.

When that happens, I collapse and just want to hit the Easy button. Maybe you relate to this. When life doesn't seem so easy, our anthem can become "It's okay—good even—to be messy." It's almost as if we say, *Well, if I can't be perfect, I'll swing in the opposite direction and quit trying.*

That's not the best response either. In fact, it can be irresponsible. That mentality draws us just as far from our purpose as perfectionism does. We live in the extremes of unrealistic expectations and limiting beliefs, falling to one end of the spectrum or the other.

If the pressure is getting to you or you're tempted to just give up, here are three proactive steps you can take right now to break through perfectionism and the pressure to prove.

1. Don't Just List Your Priorities—Do What It Takes to Live Them

My priorities should be evident by the way I live. I shouldn't have to list or explain them if I'm really living them. The same is true for you. Simply listing our top priorities is useless if our daily lives do not actually reflect them. I have to take a hard look at what I *say* are my top priorities and compare that against where my time is actually spent. A simple way to begin is by answering these questions:

- *What do I spend the most time, energy, and resources on?*
- *How well does this line up with what I say my priorities are?*
- *How can I put love into action? In other words, how can I prioritize giving love to others and receiving love myself over proving myself to people?*
- *What is the simplest, most effective thing I can do to achieve today's goals?*

2. Identify What Drives Your Perfectionism and Interrupt It

I know that the internet fuels my perfectionistic tendencies. When I look at the perfectly styled kitchen or flawless selfie, I begin to feel that I shouldn't put anything out into the world until it looks absolutely perfect. Knowing this about myself, I have to interrupt it by logging off and being present instead if I hope to do anything that matters. A simple way to replace perfectionism with purpose is to actively choose to be present wherever you are with the people right in front of you. Replace five minutes of screen time with five minutes of quality time, whether that's with your child, your spouse, a friend, or God.

My mom once advised me to engage all five senses when I'm trying to be present. Then she offered a few examples. If your kids are jumping in the leaves, don't just watch from afar, taking photos or thinking about what you must do in five minutes. Jump in with them! Feel the leaves crunch beneath your feet, breathe in and smell the crisp autumn air, and really listen to and share in the laughter of your children. If you're walking with a friend, really listen to what she's saying and engage in conversation. Take notice of the flowers you see, maybe even stopping to smell or touch them (cliché as that may sound). Focus your whole mind, body, and soul in the moment. Being fully present, even for a brief period of time, is a simple discipline that keeps my heart focused on the purpose at hand and relieves the burden of perfectionism. When I prioritize being present, I avoid living under a constant pressure to perform.

3. Make a Plan to Overcome Procrastination

Procrastination is a sign that I may be avoiding failure, and that indicates perfectionism. Take some time to consider whether you've been procrastinating instead of pursuing the dream, idea, or vision God has given you. Resolve to do one simple thing to move forward. Ask someone to hold you accountable to take this big step by a certain date. Instead of just kicking around ideas or general to-dos, declare date-based, attainable goals that will get done. If you've wanted to start a boutique, write down action steps that you will commit to complete by a set deadline. For example, "By June 1, I will have a website done and launched." Taking steps to prioritize purpose over procrastination kicks perfectionism in the pants every single time.

The bottom line? Exchange pressure for purpose by prioritizing and giving your best to whatever is in front of you. Know why? Because those precious dreams bottled up in your heart and those people in your life are privileges that should be treated as such. Never forget that faithfulness in the small things trumps striving for flawlessness in all things.

9

Overcoming Distraction with Discipline

I admit it. I am a distractible human being. I mean, sometimes the grocery store even overwhelms me. No, seriously. It has *so* many options for almost every single item. Why do we need a dozen apple varieties to choose from? That's a nightmare for an indecisive gal like me. Marigolds or Granny Smith? Honeycrisp or Golden Delicious?

This may seem silly, but if I don't go into the grocery store on a full stomach and with a list of what I need, arranged according to the store layout and my predetermined shopping loop, it takes far too long for me to make decisions. Not to mention that if I even glance at the cookie aisle, I'm a goner. Chocolate and cookies are like medicine to my soul . . . and poison that causes pimples and cavities.

Just last week I was sitting in my dentist's chair when she asked me when I'd like to come back for fillings. Yes. Fillings —plural.

What are you talking about, lady? I take great care of my teeth.

She proceeded to inform me I have five cavities. Five. The girl who's had only one cavity in her entire life, the girl who flosses as if it's her job, suddenly has five cavities. How is that possible?

I questioned her diagnosis. "Five? Are you sure about that?"

She was sure—and she asked whether I'd eaten more sugar recently.

Oh, you mean all the cookies and ice cream that snuck their way into my cart at the grocery store? How do you know about that?

I make my own diagnosis: these are not mere cavities. This is evidence of the damage that distraction causes. When I get distracted by what *looks* good, rather than staying focused on what *is* good for me, the wise decisions I intend to make go by the wayside.

And that is costly.

Why do I bring this up? Because we are a pioneering generation, one of the first generations of women who have seemingly endless opportunities at our fingertips with a little bit of grit and a Google search bar. We can easily start an Etsy store from our bedroom, apply to grad school, or try anything else that interests us. Sure, there may be obstacles along the way, but my point is that we have more options available to us than ever before—many at the touch of a button or a few swipes on our phone.

While this is a huge blessing that every single one of us should be grateful for, I know that so many feel overwhelmed by information overload or by the burden of choice.

Think about it. When you're at a buffet and *everything* looks good but your plate is only so big, what do you pick? Which is really best for you? How can you possibly narrow down the options or choose between lobster mac and the chips and guacamole?

We find ourselves with an interesting dilemma, my friend. It's definitely a good one but a challenging one nonetheless.

Perhaps in our Information Age, one of the greatest barriers to living our purpose is not a lack of opportunities but an endless list of options—what to pay attention to and where to invest our time, talent, energy, and more.

Have you ever felt that? That massive uncertainty that comes when it's time to make a decision about which major to pick, what step to take next in your career, or even how you'll spend your free time online?

When I went to college and the adviser told me to pick one major, I looked at the 257 million options and nearly handed the list back to her. *Are you kidding me? How am I supposed to do that?*

How's a girl supposed to know what she's made to do when she has a smorgasbord of options but only so much time? How must she choose only *one* that will fit her best? That just sounds like an anxiety attack waiting to happen. Unfortunately, too many options can be just as paralyzing as not enough opportunities. Instead of deciding and moving forward with one, a gal can feel so overwhelmed that she gets stuck.

When life feels uncertain or overwhelming, distractions can become a default we turn to, numbing our fears about what we're doing and where we're heading. We might indulge in one more cookie, one more minute of scrolling, or one more of something else that only damages our ability to walk toward our destiny.

What I Put in My Cart Counts

I recently read a proverb that says, "Guard your heart, for everything you do flows from it."[10]

What does that look like, practically speaking?

Well, when I go to the grocery store, I'm faced with hundreds of choices about what to put in my cart, what to stock in my refrigerator, and, ultimately, what to consume. As I've already mentioned, my decision-making abilities are severely impaired when the scent of cookies wafts in my general direction, luring me down the aisle where Little Debbie snack cakes and Chips Ahoy seem to be waiting for me!

If I'm prepared with a list that guides my decision-making, however, I usually end up making wiser choices, resisting the urge to peek down that aisle. For example, if I put spinach on my list, I put spinach in my cart. If I put spinach in my cart, that's what I consume. You don't have to be a doctor to know that spinach has several health benefits: it strengthens muscles, improves blood pressure, and boosts eyesight.

Similarly, every single day I'm faced with hundreds of choices about which voices I'm going to allow to speak into my life and dictate the direction I go. I'm faced with decisions about what I'll pay attention to and pour energy into. If I'm unprepared to make a wise decision—if I don't have a plan—I'll always be afraid of making the wrong decision and I'll end up distracted, listening to dozens of voices that may not present the healthiest choices. Distractions make me a consumer of the world rather than a contributor to the world. But the contributors are the ones who change the world.

If everything flows from our hearts, then whatever we put in our hearts and minds will inevitably influence what we do and how we live. If we feed our souls garbage, or unhealthy distractions, we'll live our daily lives without discipline or direction. When we're unprepared or don't have a plan, we can feel overwhelmed and will be much more likely to put unhealthy choices into our carts, or into our hearts, because they appeal to us in the moment.

As Benjamin Franklin once said, "If you fail to plan, you are planning to fail."

What is a better way?

Making a Distraction Action Plan

Instead of trying to ignore the inevitable distractions that pop up throughout my day, I can combat them by taking these actions:

- identifying my default distractions
- having a decision-making strategy
- equipping myself with a list

1. Identify Your Default Distractions

Based on personal experience, I believe one of the smartest things we can do is make the effort to become more self-aware. When we understand ourselves, we can get to the root of why we do certain things rather than treating the symptoms with quick fixes or to-do lists we rarely get to.

We all have our strongholds, the distractions we default to when our days overwhelm us. Like cookies, these distractions have a sneaky way of satisfying our palate. Even a moment of satisfaction can be long enough to fool us into thinking we've found what's best for us. The praise or affirmation we get by taking on a whole slew of commitments can make us feel significant and important to the people we've said yes to, even if those commitments ultimately distract us from what's most important. The entertainment or affirmation we get on social media has the power to numb our minds to what's troubling us, but it also numbs our hearts to what God is trying to tell us.

The danger of getting into default mode is that it's essentially a passive mode. A woman who lives with her soul on autopilot can't see what direction she should take. The more distracted we are, the more passive we'll become. The more passive we become, the less passionate we'll be, leaving us unable to pursue the purpose we're made for. This is exactly what we don't want to happen. We can't afford to be so bogged down with distractions that we are silent in the spaces we've been made to speak into, unable to see clearly, running about aimlessly as we try to prove ourselves instead of pressing into the lives God made us to lead.

That said, self-awareness is key to overcoming every distraction. So many of us avoid looking in the mirror and learning more about ourselves. Instead of digging deeper to see what's really going on, we distract ourselves, only worsening the problem.

Sometimes peering into the soul is a scary thing. What if I

find something I don't like? But knowing ourselves, being self-aware, is one of the greatest strengths we have against the distractions that derail us from our destiny.

For example, when I ran track in high school, I had to know both my strengths and my weaknesses if I had any hope of not only winning the races I ran but also running the right races in the first place. I was not a good distance runner, but I did have a powerful sprint. If I had been distracted by trying to keep up with the distance runners, I would have sacrificed the ability to stay in my lane, train, and run the races set out for me.

Know yourself. What distractions do you default to when life overwhelms you or when you're faced with a tough decision?

Step one is to inventory the damaging default distractions taking up space in your life so you can create the necessary disciplines to combat them.

2. Have a Decision-Making Strategy

I think sometimes we forget that distraction is not limited to social media or television. Distraction is being preoccupied with anything outside our priorities. It is time spent on minuscule tasks and unnecessary commitments that do not help move the needle in the direction we are trying to go.

I attended a conference a few months ago, and one of the speakers, who is now a dear friend of mine, mentioned how she used to struggle with what to say yes to and what to say no to. As I sat there feeling as if she was speaking to my soul, my friend taught the audience about a simple tool to use when making momentary decisions. This tool is called the 10-10-10 rule. This concept was developed by an author and speaker named Suzy Welch, and it is game changing.

The whole concept is simple. When you're faced with a decision about what you're going to spend time on or commit to, ask yourself these questions:

- *What will be the consequences of this decision in ten minutes?*
- *In ten weeks?*
- *In ten years?*

This has been so helpful for me because it encourages me to remove myself from the moment and think long term. If I say yes to something (even something small) that seems great in the moment but isn't really the best for me long term, I'll probably feel great about it in ten minutes but not so great about it in ten weeks. I might even regret it in ten years. It all boils down to drawing a decisive line by asking, *Will Future Jordan be happy that Present Jordan bought Little Debbie cakes and Doritos? Or will this only make Present Jordan happy?*

Next time you're tempted to divert your attention from the project you're working on to check Instagram or to take on another commitment because you don't want to let your friend down, try using the 10-10-10 rule to guide your decision-making process.

Make sure the big and small decisions you make are good for both Present You and Future You. When you do that, you'll set yourself up for a life full of what you're actually made to do instead of feeling bogged down by a bunch of stuff that only holds you back.

3. Equip Yourself with a List

Each daily decision we make has a greater effect than we think because small decisions add up. If I get distracted by the cookie aisle on one occasion, the effect will be relatively harmless. But as I discovered in the dentist's chair, one distraction can turn into two, three, or even more distractions that lead to more damage than I anticipated. The individual trips down the cookie aisle may not be too destructive on their own, but week after week they'll add up, and the effects on my health will be noticeable. The same is true for other distractions—and lies—we allow into our lives and make room for in our hearts. Having a guide to keep an eternal mind-set when momentary distractions begin to sneak in is important.

When I go to the grocery store and manage *not* to throw the junk that rots my teeth and clogs my arteries into my cart, it's usually because I plan ahead and have a list. I write that list *before* I'm surrounded by options so I have a guide to follow. I'm less likely to be distracted by Oreos and Doritos because my list doesn't even send me down the cookie and chip aisles.

What if we did the same thing in life? What if we had a list of what's healthy for our hearts? What would our lives look like if we woke up each day with a simple, tangible list of the directives we'll allow to guide our hearts and then stuck to that list all day, weighing our decisions against it?

That list would guide wiser decision-making, prepare us to face distractions, and allow us to walk boldly in the direction of our destiny. If we had a list, we could focus.

I encourage you to keep a simple list and to weigh against it all the demands, decisions, and distractions you're faced with each day. This isn't so much a to-do list as a *to-be* list. This is a purpose-based list that will guide you to *be* more focused, rather than distracted with unnecessary commitments.

Once you've identified your default distractions, create a list of intentional directives that will replace those defaults you turn to. Then dedicate yourself to those directives. This intentional list will help you *become* who you were made to be. The list doesn't need to be long; it simply needs to have a default directive to combat each default distraction. I'll share some of the goals on my list.

Sometimes when I'm bored, my default distraction is social media. Looking at what others are doing causes me to lose sight of where I'm heading. So I put bigger guiding goals on my list: "Be present in your marriage," "Know God and make Him known," and "Lead your team and work well." Being distracted by what others are doing doesn't align with these goals. When I look at my phone and focus on what someone else is doing, I must get back on track. I set these guiding goals, or directives, as a lock screen on my phone so that I'm consistently reminded to refocus. Each time I find myself distracted, having this as a guide helps me refocus on what matters most.

These goals are examples of what you could put on your list. There are no right or wrong answers. Keep it simple and manageable, listing one directive for each default distraction you turn to when you catch yourself going on autopilot. If you have three or four default distractions, you should have three or four clear directives to combat them. A short list is powerful because it's memorable and therefore manageable, especially if it's in a place where you'll see it often.

Every time you begin to feel overwhelmed with options, check what you're about to put in your cart—or fill up your time with—against your list. Ask yourself, *Who do I want to be, and how does this specific decision support or stifle that bigger goal?*

If that small action or choice doesn't support the woman you want to become or align with the bigger guiding goals written on your list, set it down, sister. And don't you dare feel guilty about it, not even for a second.

Part 3

What to Do Now

10

Focus on Who You Are, Not What You Do

Have you ever wondered what it really takes to live a meaningful life? More than that, do you ever catch yourself feeling overwhelmed by a thought along the lines of *What gives me meaning?*

I remember as a teenager sitting in my bedroom, which had been ever so stylishly painted hot pink and covered in zebra stripes, feeling overwhelmed by approaching life changes such as high school graduation and college applications.

The impending responsibility and decisions ahead made me look at my life and ask, *Who am I? What am I even supposed to do?* Well, at least I had the questions in the right order. I believe we must know who we are if we're ever going to discover what we are made to do.

While my faith was not yet personal (nor was it very strong), I thought perhaps it would help to ask God the questions I was wrestling with in my heart. I clearly remember looking up to heaven (well, actually it was my ceiling fan, but you know what I mean) and asking out loud, "God, who am I?"

I genuinely expected to get a response with a running list of affirmations such as, *You are a hardworking student. You are a good big sister. You are a talented athlete.* (Okay, that last one might have been a stretch.)

To my dismay, I didn't get any of those answers. In fact, I didn't get anything at first. Do you ever feel as if God sends your prayers to voice mail when an answer doesn't come right away? That's what I thought in that moment. Nevertheless, I tried again: "God, who the heck am I?"

Immediately, one single word came to my heart: *Mine.*

I was so taken aback by such a simple, profound answer that in the moment I didn't know if it was really God or just my own thoughts. I've since pondered that—for years, I might add. Looking back, as well as taking into consideration other times God has touched my heart, I'm now convinced it really was God giving me the core lesson I needed to learn for life. This one word coming to my heart was a very distinct, defining moment of my journey to understanding both myself and my Creator.

So why do I bring this up?

I bring it up because it changes everything when I understand that who I am is not based on what I do but rather on who God says I am.

Seventeen-year-old Jordan wasn't the sum of her accomplishments, titles, or labels. In fact, all that was secondary. If I believe that's true—if I actually believe that who I am holds more value than what I can prove—*shouldn't* that change everything? That one key truth gives me value, worth, authority, power, and confidence. I found my answer to life's biggest question in a dialogue so profoundly simple that many of us don't even dare to have it.

I'm not claiming to understand everything there is to know about God. In fact, I still wrestle with doubts and hard questions I'll probably never have answered. That's part of being human. That's part of faith. You can't have faith if you have all the answers.

I don't know about you, but I have seen enough evidence in my own life to know there is more to me than what I do.

The Creator of the entire universe sees me in the middle of my mess and says, "That one. She's Mine." And I believe He says the same about you.

The Antidote to Insecurity

I've been writing in a local coffee shop recently, and the other day I ran into Zach, a family friend. Round tables, big windows, and the aroma of freshly brewed coffee surrounded us as we caught up over cold brew. I told him about this book and how I was trying to piece together words that make sense, and he filled me in on some projects he and his wife, Megan, were working on.

As we talked about purpose and destiny, as well as confidence and dreams, he said something that was so simple but so profound: "We always live out of who we believe we are."

Whoa.

I stood up as I exclaimed, "That's it! That's it!"

"What's it?" he asked.

"Identity is the remedy to insecurity. It's the key to getting out of our own way and living the life we're made to live!"

If I've learned anything about myself, it's that I fail to live with purpose when I feel insecure, especially when I allow my insecurity to become my entire identity. I put myself in a box when I let my circumstances or the expectations I believe I must live up to dictate my identity and, therefore, my destiny. I lock myself inside the box of labels and limiting beliefs when statements such as "I feel insecure about _____" begin sounding more like "I *am* insecure."

When insecurity becomes an identity, we've got a major problem.

Without fail, when I forget who I truly am, I get stuck.

If I look back on times when I felt most insecure, I notice

something profound: it wasn't when I was failing but when I was on the verge of stepping into my destiny that insecurity tripped me up and held me back.

If I believe that the opposite of insecurity is a secure identity as a child of God, then actually living as though that's who I am (rather than just nodding in agreement when my pastor says so) is also a prerequisite for living with purpose.

I can do what I'm made to do only when I know who I am.

Perhaps the reason we so easily find ourselves feeling insecure is that we tend to get that backward. We try to derive our worth and identity from what we do and the labels we wear, rather than letting our lives reflect who God is in us and who He says we are.

I find it interesting how quickly and eagerly we bear the image of the world, such as by sporting a new outfit and proudly representing our favorite brands, yet how reluctant we are to fully embrace our identity.

That's where so many of us get stuck. That's why we wander about asking *What is my purpose?* when we should be asking *How can I live out of who I already am?*

When I find my identity in the things of the world—such as my circumstances, appearance, accomplishments, reputation, or status—purpose will always be out of reach because putting my identity in such places leads to insecurity.

Why? Because those are not secure places; they don't last.

Our status or circumstances might change, our accomplishments are temporary, and we cannot take our accolades with us when we breathe our last breath.

The key to overcoming insecurities, expectations, and the pressure to prove, then, is knowing and living out of our true identity.

We always live out of who we believe we are.

Stop Asking *Who Am I to* ___?

When I first started my little Etsy store from AOII's storage closet, I printed off a shipping label to send an item to a woman in Germany and thought, *Who am I to create something that someone across the world would want to buy?*

When I first spoke with my literary agent to simply learn more about the publishing process, something of which I had zero knowledge, I asked a similar question: *Who am I to write a book?*

When I was asked to speak to crowds of women, the same thought ran through my brain: *Who am I to inspire, encourage, or teach them anything?*

If you've ever asked a question like that, listen up because this is important.

While I believe it's natural to feel blown away by massive opportunities we believe we are incapable of, I think far too many of us spend way too much time living in that place of disbelief.

Instead of wrestling with the thought but giving our plan a try anyway, we get stuck there, subconsciously asking, *Who am I to make an impact? Who am I to try that business? Who am I to become a doctor? Who am I to write a book? Who am I to lead a small group?* The questions go on and on.

Then do you know what we do? Diddly-squat. Nada. Zip. Zilch. Nothing. That's what we do. We play small because we feel small—and we forget how big God is.

This again brings up impostor syndrome, which we talked about in chapter 4. This is impostor syndrome manifesting itself in how we see ourselves and our ideas, passions, dreams, and pursuits.

So here's my question: What if we stopped asking *Who am I to _____?* and instead started asking *Who am I not to _____?*

Or, rather, what if we stopped asking *Who am I to _____?* and instead started asking *Wait. Hold on. Who am I?*

If the whole idea of embracing your identity seems a little out of reach or hard to make a reality, here's my best advice: stop asking *Who am I to _____?* Instead, when you begin to feel insecure, remind yourself who you are.

I am a child of God, and nothing is impossible with my Dad.

Insecurity locks the doors. Identity—knowing who God is

in you and living as if you are who He says you are—opens them.

And remember: finding yourself will not happen when you find your purpose; knowing who you are is the key to living it out. After all, identity does so much more than tell us who we are; it reveals why we are here.

11

Redefine Success

Have you ever felt massive pressure to succeed? Or have you ever felt afraid of success, worried that if you succeeded in something, you'd end up messing it up?

Or maybe you've seen the #GirlBoss initiatives and unrealistic social media standards and experienced an odd combination of feeling both enthusiastic and overwhelmed.

I'm all about empowering women and in no way against social media, but I think with all the good that has come from these initiatives, there is also unfortunately a subtle underlying message that so many young women take from what they see in the media. My friend Kat pointed out that the subtle message is "Be everything to everyone at all times."

The problem isn't women having opportunities or making big moves. The problem is the underlying pressure women feel to prove themselves.

Women feel this pressure for likely a dozen reasons. However, because of my job I have spent quite a bit of time with young women outside my own group of friends. I've spoken with thousands of women at speaking events on campuses and at conferences all over the country, which is why I feel comfortable saying this is not merely my opinion but a widespread experience I've observed over the last few years. That said, I'm not claiming to be an expert on this, and maybe you have a different perspective.

No matter where I go, from the Deep South to the northwest corner of the country, I see a common theme among women. As I hug one after another in meet-and-greet lines, I see the exhaustion in their eyes as they tell me how much pressure they feel just trying to keep up or measure up.

Additionally, I've received countless messages online, many with the same grievance. The messages say something like, "I'm really struggling with anxiety. Sometimes I feel so much pressure to succeed at everything that I feel like I'm not enjoying anything. When I see all those empowering messages online, I feel both inspired and overwhelmed all at once. I want to be the best version of me, but sometimes it seems like I need to be 'on' at all times. It's just a lot."

I totally understand what they're feeling. I've felt it too at times. I'm a young woman in a modern society, and while I'm endlessly grateful for the opportunities I've been able to step into, I've also felt the unspoken, underlying pressure to prove myself by what I do and how I'm perceived. Rarely do I hear the message to stop the madness and instead steward the seemingly small but eternally important things in life, such as the family or relationships right in front of me. Rather, the message to do more and be more is in my face all the time. *Be more, do more, show more, and accomplish more.* In other words, prove more.

Here's what I mean: During some random Pinterest scrolling recently, I noticed a handful of pins with empowering quotes for women. One caught my eye. In big gold letters it read, "Hustle until your haters ask if you're hiring." I chuckled. How motivating is that? And catchy too. It makes me want to get up and knock it out of the park today!

But as I thought more about that quote, I realized that while the concept is strong and even motivating, the heart behind it is coming from a place of pride. At its core, this message is ultimately about proving yourself by making it to the top or becoming an object of admiration.

This makes sense, I suppose. That's what the world tells us to do! Prove the haters wrong. Outrun everybody else. *Ohhh yeah.* That's when we'll succeed, right?

Maybe not.

Don't get me wrong. I hope you have a work ethic. Hustling—working hard—is good in itself, but I've discovered that when I hustle because I feel the need to prove something to the world (or to myself), I can get caught up in the hustle itself and lose the *heart* behind what I'm doing.

When I lose the heart, I forget my "why," and that's a disaster. That's when we begin to replace excellence with the pressure to meet expectations. That's when we get stuck and end up totally stressed out.

As I said, I'm all about encouraging women to give their absolute best. However, I've learned the hard way that there's a difference between striving to *be* the best and simply giving our best.

The woman who draws her worth, purpose, and power from her status or other people's opinions of her will always be a slave to the pressure to be the best. If she can keep up, she'll be admired, and she might be celebrated and praised, but I'll be honest—when I feel pressure to live up to what the world says is powerful, impressive, and admirable, I forget what really matters most.

Maybe you can relate. Maybe you're the stressed-out student barely able to keep up, the tired mama just wanting some downtime, or the lonely woman completely wrecked by a recent rejection. Maybe you feel stuck behind your own insecurities, not sure how to push past them. Maybe when you look at women admired by the world, women who are living out some grand and impressive dreams, you feel small, insignificant, unseen, or unheard.

With all the messaging to be our best selves at all times, it can be hard to find a place where we have any breathing room at all. In fact, I don't think we can be our best selves if we never pause to eat, drink, and see that our work is good.[11] Additionally, the pressure to succeed at everything people see can take away from the ability to truly be successful in the places that are unseen.

Truthfully, I used to think that the only women God uses for big things are missionaries saving lives overseas or women who get on stage in front of crowds. I didn't immediately think of the tired woman scrubbing a frying pan in her kitchen sink and fighting back tears after a long day, or the faithful woman struggling to pay rent, or the young girl recovering from an unexpected breakup.

That changed when I began to study the stories of women God used to do world-changing things. Women like Esther, Ruth, and Mary. Seriously, I encourage you to read their stories. They weren't setting out to be rock stars. They weren't trying to keep up with what other women were doing. They weren't at the top of their MLMs, leading multimillion-dollar companies, or posting selfies from their fancy jobs in big cities.

You know what those girls were doing? They were showing up for their everyday realities. They were being ordinary, simple human beings with nothing to prove but everything to give. The difference between them and us? They didn't have all the noise. They had space to listen to what God was trying to get through to them. They actually did what He said, and He took care of the rest. They had influence because they focused on impact. They just showed up instead of trying to show off.

When we always have something to prove, we close ourselves off to protect our image and end up making everything about us. But guess what? The world does not revolve around you and me, sister. However, when we have everything to give, when we stop trying to show off and just start showing up to what God has for us, even when that risks our reputation, we can discover a meaningful life.

From reading these women's stories, I've learned that the art of living with purpose right where I am begins when I let go of my pride and redefine success.

The pressure is off when I accept the fact that I won't always fit the mold of who the world, the church, or other people expect me to be. I won't always measure up to someone else, and maybe that's okay. Nine times out of ten, I won't finish first, make it to the top, or appear to be on my A game.

But guess what? That does not mean I'm not successful. That does not mean I cannot live a meaningful life.

Why? Because deep inside is a purpose fueled by an everyday kind of passion. It doesn't come from the big, impressive things I've done but through the small, ordinary things as seemingly insignificant as joining that sorority back in college, sitting on an old hand-me-down couch and swapping stories with the man who would later become my husband, and hugging the girl behind the cash register when she reveals she's had a rough week.

The unrecorded moments. The unseen surrenders. The uncertain yeses I gave that led to unknown places, leaving me completely undone in the very best way, free of all the labels and lies I've spent so much time wrapping around myself. These are what give me purpose.

Stop Saying "Goals"; Start Setting Goals

I've observed something over the last few years of working online: people today seem to spend more time commenting "goals" on social media posts that seem to embody the ideal than they do setting goals to get to where they want to go. Perhaps we need a strategy for setting goals that is truly effective in everyday life. Before I dive into that, I think it's important that I put this out there: my goal is not merely to have a happy life. My goal is to live a meaningful life. That kind of life requires that I go through some seasons that don't feel so happy. Of course, I want to experience happiness as well as success, but I do not want to be too focused on some made-up ideal. More than anything, I want to be intentional.

I don't know about you, but I refuse to live my life based on certain conditions or outcomes (and I hope you do too). Unfortunately, far too many girls believe that until they get a certain job or unless they do any number of other things, they'll miss out on their purpose.

Do you know what living with that mind-set is? It is living a life driven by pressure, not by purpose. If you live like that, you'll be more unsuccessful than if you never got that job or that guy or whatever else it is you think your dreams depend on.

Sister, please redefine how you look at success.

What if you stopped looking at it as this big jackpot you have to win and instead saw it as little wins that happen when you focus on being who God made you to be? Instead of defining success only as something based on your future, your career, or your accomplishments, consider how you might be able to succeed every single day if you simplify how you define it.

If you created micro-success factors, or doable daily goals, you'd be equipped to succeed at life every day (which, I believe, would be motivation to continue improving and growing!). For example, micro-success factors for me include these daily goals:

- I will be off my phone and will spend quality time with my husband by 6:00 p.m.

- I will move my body for thirty minutes.
- I will talk to God.
- I will write one thousand words.

What if we simplified how we viewed success so that every day felt not like a waiting game but instead like an intentional day on the path to walking out the life we're made for?

My challenge to you is to take your eyes off all the success and status symbols online and consider what success looks like in your personal life. Define it on both a macro and micro level.

First, go big. What has God put on your heart to do in a big way? What fires you up? What dream or idea seems totally crazy in the very best way? Write those big ideas and goals down.

Then, go small. Focus on the ways you can find success every day. What micro-success factors, or daily goals, would make each day feel like an achievement, propelling you closer to those bigger goals? In addition to writing down the big stuff, write down your micro-success factors and stick them on your mirror or set them as a wallpaper on your phone.

Having faith and following through on these simple disciplines can be critical to bringing the bigger goals to fruition. These micro-success factors not only will help you live a more intentional life each day but also will serve as the action plan to get you from point A to point B when it comes to those bigger dreams. You can't have one without the other.

Micro-success factors and daily disciplines matter because they add up. If you can go to bed every single night and see the day as a success, you're going to be less bogged down by the pressure to prove and more able to make progress toward what you're made to do.

12

Let It Go, Girl

I want you to do a really honest inventory of your life for a second. Is it possible that you have unhealthy habits or comforts in your life that you hold on to, even if only by a thread? I know I do. This became all the more obvious to me recently when a friend and I sat cross legged on the floor, catching up, swapping stories, and snacking on crackers and cheese.

At one point she opened up about her past addiction to Adderall, a prescription drug designed to treat attention deficit disorder. She explained how she felt when she took it: productive, confident, and energized. But when it wore off and she crashed? She felt sluggish, empty, and irritable. She craved a life full of authentic passion and purpose, but she felt that in her truest, rawest form, she was nothing without the drug.

"I used the drug so much that it nearly replaced my need

for God," she shared, laying her soul scars right out there in the open. "No wonder I didn't feel close to Him. I was dependent on what I thought brought me life, not on the Author of my life."

Well, shoot dang, girlfriend. That's deep.

I began to wonder whether I also depended on some things for life outside of the Author of life.

She went on. "It filled me with a temporary sense of confidence and control, until it eventually wasn't enough. I knew something had to change because I really didn't need the drug. One day I decided to dump out all the pills but keep the prescription just in case I wanted it again. But as I held the bottle over the trash can, I realized if I was going to let go, if I was really going to change, I had to let go 100 percent, not 99 percent."

Sister was speaking to my soul.

We can't be 99 percent free and call that freedom. We can't move forward through the door of our destiny if we're still holding on to comforts or things we use to compensate for our lack of confidence.

This reminds me of a quote that says, "Old ways won't open new doors." In other words, if we don't let unhealthy habits go, the growth we hope to experience won't come.

As my friend learned, living with purpose begins with releasing the comforts that have a hold *on* us so God can do a work *in* us. She had to release her dependence on the drug to experience real and raw passion and confidence.

This transition season brought about her transformation, developing real inner strength inside her. Transformation means changing from the inside out—experiencing change at the core of who we are, which then changes our behavior and circumstances.

You want to know what that means? It means we must *be changed* on the inside so we can *be the change* in the world. And that often begins with making a hard choice—a choice to make a change when it comes to what we cling to for courage, comfort, or confidence. It begins with doing the hard work that's required to let go of what has a hold on us—and not most of it but all of it.

What's my point here? It's that you and I can break through the barriers that hold us back only if we break *away* from all the unhealthy things that have a hold on us. The door to our destiny gets stuck when we refuse to release the 1 percent we cling to.

Get Real with Yourself

I'll be honest. When I first thought about what I might be holding on to personally, nothing came to mind. So I didn't think I had anything to share with you.

Then a few months ago, my husband and I decided we wanted to go to marriage counseling—not because our marriage was falling apart but because we both realized it would be a healthy discipline to strengthen our marriage.

Matt describes marriage counseling as preventative maintenance and compares it to getting the oil changed on your car. You don't get your oil changed after your car breaks down. You do it to prevent your car from breaking down so you can get to where you want to go, right?

If we take care of our cars like this, why wouldn't we take care of ourselves, our marriages, and our health in the same way? In other words, this mind-set can be applied to counseling in general, not just marriage counseling.

This discipline has been incredibly helpful in these early years of marriage. In our first meeting I discovered unmet expectations I'd been holding on to that I didn't even realize were there! Turns out Matt had some unmet expectations he'd held on to as well. We opened up, we prayed, and we confessed everything we had unknowingly been holding on to. It was so healing.

Did you know that when you hold on to something like unmet expectations, you actually set yourself up to be bitter without even meaning to? Once I identified these expectations, I was able to let go of them for the very first time. Immediately I felt lighter. I found that I was more patient and understanding. Identifying and letting go of unmet expectations proved to be pivotal, and I believe it has really improved our marriage.

Sister, no matter what it is you might be holding on to—something not so obvious, like unmet expectations, or something incredibly difficult, like addiction—counseling can be so helpful. Unfortunately, many people avoid it because they think they have to be falling apart or at rock bottom.

My advice if you're struggling with the idea of seeking counsel is this: shift your mind-set. Don't be afraid to make an uncomfortable choice so you can experience positive change.

Something Has to Die

I know that subhead sounds awfully morbid. Allow me to explain. As I'm writing these words, I'm watching summer turn to fall outside my window. It's that long-anticipated, marvelous time of the year when the soybean fields change from green to golden brown, warm air turns crisp, people gather for weekend bonfires and football tailgates, and every U-Pick apple orchard in the Indiana countryside is filled with families and friends. If you've never experienced fall in Indiana, I can assure you that you're missing out. (I know I said FOMO is fake a few chapters back, but this is the exception.)

Anyway, I just brewed a cup of tea, and I'm curled up on my paisley office chair. An apple pie–scented candle is burning in the kitchen, really setting the mood. The leaves outside my big office window have started to turn beautiful shades of yellow, red, and orange. Days like this bring back childhood memories of being at a local apple farm with Grandma and Grandpa and of snuggling into Grandma as we'd take a tractor ride through the cornfields, enjoying the colorful leaves on the nearby sunlit trees.

Anyway, watching the occasional leaf fall to the ground makes me realize something I hadn't before. For months the leaves were vibrant green and full of life, shading the sidewalks and our backyard. You'd think they would have found their calling when they were at their best—bright, glossy, and alive.

Then, at just the right time, they begin to change color. They're beautiful, but when they flutter through the wind as they float to the ground, when they create a canvas across the tree line, dancing in the breeze as they go, they're dead.

Maybe transformation can be hard because, although it's a beautiful and necessary process, something must die for it to occur.

The good news is we get more leaves in the spring. After a long, cold winter, new life buds on every branch. This cycle of flourishing, then withering, and then flourishing again has been built into the trees' design. That same process—release and resilience—is built into us too.

We must let go of something—our pride, an old habit, a

comfortable sin, or something else we cling to just a little too tightly. This is a difficult, often uncomfortable, and sometimes even painful part of finding the power, purpose, and freedom we were made to live with.

Personally, I'm not a fan of seasons that force me to make a hard choice or release my favorite comforts. I don't do well with change, I guess. Maybe I get my resistance to change from my dad, the man who's slept his entire adult life with the same pillow he had in college and has now lovingly nicknamed Lumpy.

Lumpy the pillow. I know. It sounds ridiculous. Who would hold on to something so old? Maybe someone who's resistant to releasing what's familiar, someone who would rather avoid change. To us, Lumpy may seem gross, but to my dad, it brings comfort and consistency.

We all like comfort, consistency, and control, don't we?

You may not have a lumpy old pillow, but I bet you're hanging on to other lumpy old things in your life—things that may promise life and bring you comfort but ultimately can't deliver and quite possibly even hold you back from doing what you've been designed to do.

Back to the leaves.

Imagine if the leaves never let go. We'd never get to gaze at the vibrant autumn hues or leap into the piles of raked leaves that hold a hint of the magic of childhood.

But the leaves don't cling to the tree. They don't refuse to budge. They surrender to the design and submit to the process—the purpose that's been built into them since seasons began. The tree flourishes only when the dead parts are removed so new life can grow, and it can foster new growth only when the root system is healthy.

The same is true for you and me. We can be resilient through the difficult seasons and bounce back when we let something unhealthy go, but we must have healthy roots beneath the surface. When our hearts are healthy, we can fearlessly make the hard choice to shed whatever needs to be removed so we can experience real, lasting change. We flourish only when we release control of the lifeless things we've held on to, the things that suck the life out of us, choke the health of our hearts, and hold us back from living as we should.

What lifeless things are you holding on to? What do you need to release? An unhealthy habit? An old flame you keep going back to against your better judgment? A grudge you've been carrying? Something else?

Sister, this can be a process. The leaves don't change colors, drop from branches, and bud again all on the same day. And neither do we. I know that deep-seated issues such as addiction, PTSD, self-harm, and other battles with mental health are not just dropped overnight. If you struggle with something like this, please seek the necessary professional help.

You're not being weak. Choosing to address the issue you

are facing requires strength and purpose. No matter what you are struggling with or how long it takes to completely release it, do not give up. You and I must take steps to let go of what poisons our fruit and stifles our growth if we wish to bloom as we've been made to.

I'm with you on this, friend. Let today be the day you choose to make a change.

13

Get Out of Your Own Way

know I've talked a lot about pressure throughout these pages, but I want to park here and dive a little deeper for a second. I want to talk about it because I see so many girls like me living with this endless pressure to find the dreamy guy or land that perfect job or create a cool business. Oh, and it all needs to happen ASAP, right?

Then I sometimes see one of two things happen:

1. A gal gets that job, does a happy dance, packs up her car, and drives across the country while rocking out to Taylor Swift, convinced she's made it in life. Then she starts that job, but within a few months it turns out not to be at all what she expected. Or the business she was so eager to start sucks up all her time and stresses her out

beyond a level she signed up for. Or the guy she
originally thought was Mr. Right turns out to be
Mr. Wrong. *Mega bummer.*

2. She is so wrapped up in the pressure to strike gold
on try number one that she misses the good stuff.
She expects that first job out of college, her first go
at trying a business, or the next guy she dates to be
all she could ever want. She winds up feeling so
paralyzed by perfectionism and unrealistic expectations that she doesn't apply for the job or give the
nice guy a chance. Or she believes she's unqualified
to try her hand at something new and as a result
just sits on her booty. Or, worse, she doesn't give
herself grace if she misses the target on her first try.

Sound familiar?

Sister, hear me when I say this (because I've learned from
personal experience): it won't always be your first or your second
or even your third try that you land on your thing.

Life comes in phases. You don't have to have it all figured
out, land your dream job, or find what you'll do for the rest of
your life in this decade of your life.

You will never, ever grow or learn the lessons each step of
the journey is meant to teach you if you focus only on how that
step could be a waste of time. You'll never take a risk or say

hello to a stranger if you're always afraid there could be something or someone better out there. I mean, holy cow, just stop the madness!

Don't mistake taking the pressure off as a free pass to abandon drive or intentionality. But please, for the sake of your own sanity, take off the pressure to strike gold on your first try. Every step molds you, shapes you, and makes you grow. Isn't that what life is really all about anyway? Isn't that growth the gold we're looking for?

Pressure-Breaking Strategies

As I mentioned in the introduction, when I begin to feel the pressure to prove myself, I have to look deeper. I need to consider where that pressure is really coming from. If I'm honest, it's usually coming from inside. That doesn't mean external pressures don't exist, but it does mean the choice to internalize those pressures and operate in response to them is on me.

With that in mind, I have to take responsibility and address the pressure I experience if I want to live my purpose. Up until this point, we've talked a lot about the problems living under pressure can create. However, I don't want to leave you without explaining the strategies that have helped me tackle the pressure:

1. Remove or retreat from high-pressure influences.
2. Quit avoiding awkwardness and everyday opportunities.
3. Shift your perspective.

Dive into each of these with me.

1. Remove or Retreat from High-Pressure Influences

I used to follow some people online that I thought were motivating me. To a degree, they were. However, I began to realize that by following their lives and listening to the constant message to be more, do more, and try harder, *motivation* began to be replaced by *pressure*—pressure to keep up and make myself as successful or fit or interesting as they are.

That is super exhausting and honestly not all that healthy.

If you feel pressure to prove that you're a good wife or a good Christian or a successful student or career woman—just for the sake of proving that you are—please do me a favor: *think about what you're allowing into your mind.* What messages are you filling your life with? What do you spend time doing, and what are you consumed with? Who are you listening to? Is it life giving and intentional? Or draining and exhausting?

It's one thing to be equipped and inspired to grow, set goals, and make positive change. It's another thing to be exhausted trying to keep up with what the culture dictates or other people's expectations of who you should be or what you should do.

So if people you follow online make you feel all sorts of pressure, don't blame them. Blame yourself for continuing to follow them when doing so makes you turn your life into a race to keep up. Solution? Just unfollow them. Remove those influences, even if only temporarily, until you are able to refocus on the reason you're doing something rather than on the pressure to keep up with what everyone else seems to be doing.

Or if someone in your life pressures you to do things you don't want to do—or makes you feel inadequate unless you do or achieve certain things—you have to either back away from that relationship or look for a lot more balance. For example, if that voice is a relative (such as a parent), I don't suggest cutting this person out of your life; he or she likely has your best interests in mind. However, if you have one voice that puts a whole lot of pressure on you or just seems to be the loudest, please seek out some more uplifting and positive voices to balance that one out.

It is your responsibility to regulate the voices you listen to.

2. Quit Avoiding Awkwardness and Everyday Opportunities

I've often observed that when I press in to be closer to people, I feel far less pressure to prove anything to them. Nearness has a beautiful way of nixing the need to prove ourselves.

I remember one time I learned this lesson so vividly and personally. I was sitting on a bus-stop bench in my college town one chilly evening when I noticed that the young woman sitting on the same bench looked sad and lonely. It's always awkward, isn't it, when it's just you and one other person in a small space—sitting at a bus stop, standing in an elevator, or passing in a narrow hallway?

Five minutes elapsed, and neither of us had said a word. (How can we just coexist with people and pretend they're not there?) The bus must have been delayed, because a few more minutes passed in silence.

Finally, I couldn't take it anymore, and I spoke up. I introduced myself, and she told me her name—her American name, anyway. In broken English, Nancy shared that she'd been in the United States for two years, working on her PhD.

Intrigued, I asked about her experience. She was shy, but I kept asking questions, and somewhere along the line she mumbled, "I spend a lot of time alone."

I stopped in my tracks.

"Wait. Haven't you made *any* friends here?" I asked, just to verify what she'd said.

"Not really, other than my roommate. No one really talks to me."

How was that possible? She'd been in the States two years, and no one had reached out to her?

I asked for her phone number and whether she'd like to get lunch sometime.

Her eyes widened, and she barely got her words out. "You? And me? You want to go to lunch with me?"

"Yes! Of course!"

Over the next several months, I spent many afternoons visiting with Nancy, learning about her culture, hearing stories about her childhood, and listening to all the dreams bottled up in her heart—most of which had little to do with her PhD.

I loved it. It was life giving, and I always looked forward to our time together. As we shared meals and worked through English vocabulary to communicate better, I taught her about American history and traditions. Through many conversations over hot tea, I could tell she had been storing up her stories for years, just waiting for someone willing to listen.

I found so much purpose and joy in those not-so-ordinary hours with her.

One day at a little corner bakery, I had a passing thought: What if world-changing purpose was profoundly simple? What if simply seeing and serving people—showing up and listening—is the secret ingredient to purpose? What if friendship is what is needed to break down barriers and open doors to what we've been made for?

The more I got to know Nancy, the more I saw so much of myself in her despite our different upbringings. We all just want to be seen. We're all just longing to be loved. Isn't that why we want to find our purpose? Why we crave meaning, significance, and affirmation?

The hard reality, though, is that we might not always be seen. We might sit on a bus-stop bench alone, night after night, awkwardly ignoring the opportunity to step into purpose because we hope someone else will speak first. I fear we've become so afraid of feeling awkward that we avoid opening the door to opportunity and stepping outside our comfort zones.

Since then, our journeys have taken Nancy and me in different directions. Yet those months we spent getting to know each other taught me something huge about life and purpose: it comes down to being willing to be uncomfortable, get outside ourselves, meet others where they are, and make room.

There's something marvelous in that. It doesn't require big performances or perfect report cards. We simply need willing hearts and open doors. Yet we're so quick to build up our lives and our résumés and, inevitably, our walls. Maybe our challenge, then, is to build backward. When we learn to break down walls and open doors, making room for strangers and outsiders, the connections we build topple the barriers we don't even know are holding us back.

I recently read a quote by a writer named Claire Gibson that resonated with me:

Is it possible that there is no such thing as a stranger? Is it possible that all the borders we draw are invisible? Is it possible that the lines of language and skin color and difference are passing away? . . . I'm struck by how much harder it is for me to welcome in those "close" strangers who are a regular part of my life. The sister-in-law who doesn't quite fit in. The mother who doesn't live up to my needs or expectations. Sometimes emotional boundary lines are harder to cross than oceans.[12]

You know what that tells me? It tells me that pressure is replaced by purpose when we make room for those who are completely different from us. People who don't think like us, talk like us, or look like us. I mean, that's what Jesus did, right?

What if we did that too? Purpose isn't in pressure but in pressing in. Awesome things can come from being willing to push past a little awkwardness. Try it sometime.

3. Shift Your Perspective

A friend recently put it to me in a question: "What are you doing to bring heaven to earth *today*?"

Well, wow. That makes it simple, doesn't it? We don't need a lot of money or an impressive résumé to make that happen. We just need willing hearts—not even to make the entire world a better place but simply to help make one person's world a better place.

Living a life of purpose starts with standing up and starting small. I have to trust God and step toward people, not away from them. True purpose is more about understanding than being understood. Friendship is more about seeing than being seen. It is more about serving than being served.

It's really very simple. When we show up to do what we think we can't do and reach out to those we don't understand, everything changes. This may look like volunteering, trying something new, taking a meal to a friend, calling and apologizing when you'd rather not, inviting someone you normally wouldn't, or donating more than you think you can afford.

So the question we ought to be asking isn't *What is my purpose?* but *How can I bring heaven to earth, right here today?*

This doesn't have to be so complicated. A woman breaks through the pressure to prove when she gets outside herself and just loves people. She brings heaven to earth when she chooses to love the mess out of people instead of wallowing in her mess. Yes, a girl driven by her purpose has to take care of herself and chase her dreams, but she doesn't stop there. She invites in the outcasts and difficult ones—even before her own dreams come true.

Do you see how uncomplicated this can be? A life that is free of pressure is possible only when we choose to show up right where we are—not after we fool ourselves into thinking we've got life figured out. When we shed our expectations and instead open our eyes to what's right in front of us, make room for those around us, and get over the awkwardness inside us, the pressure fades and purpose comes into play.

If you take nothing else away from this chapter, please remember this: the more you press into serving others and building meaningful relationships, the less you'll feel the pressure to prove yourself to people whose opinions don't really matter.

14

Stop Waiting, Start Living

once had someone reach out to me online and ask, "How do I handle it when it feels like I'm in a perpetual season of waiting?"

That hit me right in the soul. I know that feeling all too well.

For so long, it felt as though my life was all about getting to some desired destination ahead.

Puberty? No, thanks. Can I just come out on the other side, blossomed like a beautiful butterfly already? Breakups? Healing? Hard decisions? SOS. Where's the Easy button through this stuff?

When I was in high school, I just wanted to get to college. Of course, after a few years in college, I wanted nothing more than to grab that degree, toss my cap, and settle into a comfortable job. When Matt and I got engaged and had a fourteen-month engagement, those last few months before the wedding felt like a never-ending waiting game. I just wanted to be married already!

I could give you 1,004 examples, but I'm sure you get the point.

Maybe you feel as if you're in a perpetual season of waiting too. Maybe you've been waiting to finally meet "the one," find out if you were accepted into grad school, get pregnant, or make a certain amount of money so you'll never have to worry about finances again.

I don't know what you're waiting for, but I do know that if you're focused on what you're waiting for, chances are you're wasting the opportunity to live life to the fullest right where you are.

Why are we sitting around waiting for some magical day when it'll all suddenly just click for us? Why do we make our purpose in life contingent upon a certain milestone, accomplishment, outcome, or opportunity?

I mean, really.

Be honest with yourself: What is your mind-set toward unfigured-out seasons? If you look at today as a day to *get through* instead of a day to *live through,* or if you always look at your future as something to figure out, you are going to be incredibly dissatisfied with your life. Not only that, but you will also be walking 1,000 percent out of line with your purpose.

Stop Trying to Fast-Forward Your Life

A few weeks ago, my husband and I started watching one of those home-makeover shows on television. To my surprise, it taught me something I wasn't expecting to learn from daytime TV.

In one episode the makeover team had to demolish nearly half the house they were working on. They had to strip it down to just the framework before any of the planned updates and renovations could take place. I sat on the couch and watched intently as the demo crew took sledgehammers to the old drywall and scraper tools to the chipped paint on the exterior. They also ripped up the floorboards one at a time. By the time the demolition was done, it'd be a stretch to call what was left of the place a house.

I couldn't wait to see the final product. My favorite part of these shows is comparing the "before" and "after" photos, because sometimes I get a little impatient during the in-between. When sawdust is flying, walls are being busted down, or the roof caves in, it can be hard to imagine that something even better will come of the mess. Sometimes I'd prefer to just fast-forward to the "after" photos instead of sitting through the process—not just when I watch home-improvement shows but also in life.

When we find ourselves in difficult or long seasons, it can

be tempting to wish them away and skip to the next thing. Perhaps that's because we've become so used to getting answers in an instant. Gone are the days when we have to wonder about a question someone brings up at dinner, even something as preposterous as "Who first discovered you could milk cows?" (As you can imagine, my friends and I have some interesting conversations.) But it's true! We can have answers in seconds with a quick search on our smartphones. We can make a reservation for dinner in an instant with a touch of a button, and we can receive what we ordered online in a matter of hours thanks to Amazon Prime.

But what about when the raw realities of life don't allow such a luxury? When we don't get to the desired destination, land on the right answer, or see the reason something hasn't happened as quickly as we'd like?

When something incredibly sad occurs or we face rejection or disappointment, it can be hard to believe something better and more beautiful can come from the rubble. And if we take our eyes off our ultimate purpose or forget why we started, we risk identifying more with the mess than with the message it's teaching us.

The problem? We often turn long, hard seasons full of uncomfortable change into something to endure rather than something to enjoy because of what we can learn. Something to wish away instead of something to celebrate. We anticipate the next season with eagerness. When it doesn't come fast enough, we fixate on our unmet expectations instead of on the holy invitation to see the purpose *even in this*—even in the waiting, the breaking down, and the long and awkward road to becoming who God made us to be. We fail to see who we can reach, how we can love, and even what we can let go of *right here* and instead focus on getting *over there*.

Maybe you desperately want to fast-forward through hard seasons, bypass the discomfort that comes with change, and just get to the "good stuff" already. I get that. I'm guilty of this too. But let me tell you: this *is* the good stuff. Just because you're not at your desired destination does not mean you are unable to live out your destiny right here on the divine middle ground.

Doing anything worthwhile with our lives requires that we go through the process, not around it. Consider the home-renovation show. Although the demolition was messy, leaving the house looking hopelessly broken, the crew still finished the project. I didn't once see them toss their hammers aside, look at the heaps of rubble, and say, "Oh no! What have we done? We're doomed!"

Their response was quite the opposite. The demo crew was excited, and they high-fived one another after a hard day's work. They knew what would happen and were prepared for it, and they celebrated the progress. Even when it looked like a step backward, they knew it was truly a step forward. Even when they discovered issues with the foundation and other challenges, they solved the problems and powered through. They continued to show up daily with hands ready to work and eventually completed the project (and I got to enjoy my beloved "after" photos).

Think about it: What gave them the energy to finish the project? Why were they able to power through even after they discovered problems? They were driven by purpose, motivated by the project they had set out to complete, not sidetracked or defeated by the problems along the way.

When I look at my life through this lens, I learn something powerful. When I'm driven by my purpose, I can persevere and even appreciate the demolition because I know it's only a small part of a much bigger story. But when I'm focused on my problems, operating from a place of fear and anxiety, trying to avoid any further challenges, I run the risk of being trapped in my own head.

Let me put this to you straight: you and I can't afford to let temporary circumstances dictate our eternal purpose. We must allow the eternal purpose to infuse our temporary circumstances. Our purpose must breathe life into every circumstance if we hope to be content, confident, and capable of doing important things.

I have to keep my purpose in mind and trust that God knows what He's doing as He works on me, even when I reach stages in that process that seem undesirable. Each time I feel overwhelmed by disappointments and other demolition in life, I have to shift my focus and remind myself that God has put me here and brought me to this point on purpose, for a purpose.

Demolition is part of the preparation. Preparation and perseverance make the "after" pictures possible. And guess what? God is making a masterpiece out of you, friend. Don't be afraid of a little mess along the way.

If you find yourself in a season of waiting, don't quit. I know it can be so easy to wish it away, pray for a quick fix, or think the answer lies in some future outcome.

I hate to break it to you, but you can't Amazon Prime your life. You can't make it go any faster than it's going to go. You can't fast-forward the story that's being written for you or rush through the hard work that might be required of you right now.

It just doesn't work like that.

Thank goodness too, or we'd all be Amazon Priming everything we don't like, only to wake up one day and realize we're eighty and lived half our life on fast-forward.

I don't want that to be my story. I want to live my story, even the hard and long and messy days. And holy moly, I hope and pray you do too, because those are the days that will shape you.

Your purpose isn't something you'll find when the seemingly endless wait is over. Your purpose exists and unfolds in the process. You can't make this story go any faster than it is, but you can decide if you'll show up and live it even when it doesn't go according to plan.

Please don't waste your one precious life because you've bought into the lie that you're in a perpetual season of waiting and still have to find your purpose. That is simply untrue and so not the type of life God has in mind for you.

Make This Your Mantra

Proverbs 31:25 is one of my favorite verses. It says that a woman who fears the Lord faces the future with laughter, not fear. Without meaning to, Nana, in her own silly way, showed me how to do that.

When I think about her—the way she dared me to face problems, challenges, and insecurities—I don't think of a woman who was paralyzed with fear or worried about what others thought of her. I think of a woman who danced as if she knew her destiny had nothing to do with whatever discouragement or other demolition life threw her way. She would know too. That woman lived a hard story, from selling her wares on the streets in Mexico as a young child to tragically losing her husband to a massive heart attack as they dined in a restaurant in Mexico City.

A widow and an immigrant to the United States with four young children, she was the definition of a gal who turned her cannots into cans.

In simpler ways she taught me to do this too.

Every time I was faced with something I didn't want to do as a child, even something as simple as apologizing to my baby brother or finishing a boring homework assignment, she'd do a little dance, sing a silly tune, and finish it off by plopping onto the couch with a smile and raising her arms up to heaven as she belted out a big "Ta-da!" That always made me laugh. She never failed to give me the boost I needed to step into the challenge before me, no matter how big or small.

Nana didn't just teach me to take big steps of faith. She also showed me how to dance into those big steps with light in my heart and laughter in my soul. It was as if in all these moments when I felt afraid and unsure, she saw beyond the fear and insecurities into the bold, brave, purposeful heart God gave me. And by example, she gave me the courage to let myself live like a woman with that kind of heart, right where I am.

The world tells us, "Once you [get that job, heal from that wound, figure out that problem], you can start living your purpose."

However, a girl who knows how to shove that lie to the side, peel off the labels, and kick limiting beliefs like that in the butt lives with purpose before a single thing is set up or secured.

I want you to be able to live like that kind of girl. So I wrote a little declaration for you to speak out loud and take with you long after you close this book. Feel free to highlight the lines that resonate with you most, tear it out, and put it somewhere you'll see it. This is for you:

I might not be where I want to be, but I am where I'm supposed to be. My circumstances don't define me. I'll press on past the pressure to prove because God made me on purpose for a purpose. I'll choose to see people. I'll share my story even before I get to the happy ending. I'll give my gifts away instead of just looking for my gift. Instead of avoiding failure, I'll bravely step into the fun of the adventure. I'll be a culture changer instead of being changed by the culture. I'll celebrate the beauty of this season and the challenges that come with change. I'll embrace the waiting, and in the middle of it, I'll love people with a heart of intentional purpose.

I have found that when I live each day with this as my motivating anthem, I stop being so freaked out by all the dreams I don't have figured out yet. It grounds me, reminds me of what truly matters, and helps me live with purpose before anything else is figured out. I want this for you too. Make this your mantra. We can use it to get out of our own heads and back to opening our arms to the world around us, where we are, with what we have, even before we make a perfect plan.

Unfigured-Out Dreams Might Be the Best Kind of Dreams

I want to make a proposition. I propose that unfigured-out dreams may be the very best kind, as frustrating as they can be. Why? Because maybe the less we try to figure out the future, the more we can be really intentional in the present.

I'd even argue that this day, right now, this very season of unfigured-outed-ness might be the very best thing for you. I believe even our hardest days can sometimes be the best things for us. Think about that. Would you be who you are today without the rough patches and hard seasons that shaped you?

I doubt it.

Embrace these days, whatever they look like for you. You are a big girl. Instead of pouting about what you can't control, learn to implement discipline and intentionality in things you can control. You can decide to make your bed each morning.

You can get over your pride and ask for help. You can choose to quit gossiping, remove yourself from drama, or be kind to that difficult person in your life.

Please don't be so obsessed with figuring out your dreams that you overlook the opportunity to live like the girl you see in your dreams right now—the girl who is compassionate, confident, joyful, secure in her identity, and able to influence people wherever she goes. Live like that now, before it's all figured out.

Don't be so focused on figuring it out or landing a dream job that you don't give yourself the freedom to step into all that is in this season.

Remember how I said that I had no idea writing a book was even a dream of mine? I had no idea that it'd be an avenue I'd get to use to carry out my big purpose.

That big purpose? Love God and love people.

If I stay rooted in that, the pressure surrounding anything else I do is off. I have the freedom to enjoy the journey as I try new things and influence others along the way.

Saying yes to simply stepping out and trying my hand at a little shop, which evolved into a blog, which then turned into so much more, was the best decision I ever made. I had to take a chance with a little risk and push apprehension and what-ifs aside long enough to give it a try.

Stop tripping yourself up, sis. It's really so, so simple.

Keep your heart, mind, and eyes open. You never know when your next yes will be the best step you've ever taken.

Fail Forward

There's one last thing you should know.

When Nana first taught me to take big steps, my legs were still weak, and I often fell. I fell back when I looked back, and I lost my balance and tumbled to the side when I looked to the left or right. But when I looked forward and kept my eyes fixed on what was ahead, I could fall and still be moving forward. I could lose my footing, but I didn't stay down for long. Nana always helped me up. Then I'd again set my gaze on where I was headed.

My charge to you? Stop looking to the left and right, trying to find a purpose that isn't lost. Quit looking back, believing that you haven't come far enough or that you somehow messed it up already.

Remember what we talked about in chapter 4? Quit avoiding or merely expecting failure and instead start *preparing* for it. As long as you're prepared and looking forward, you might just fumble into unexpected dreams when you "fail" at what you thought you were supposed to do.

Insecurities, expectations, and the pressure to prove will be barriers between you and the life you're made for only if you allow them to be.

Your purpose will come to life if you give yourself permission to put your full yes on the table and take a step forward, even when you'd rather take a seat.

So I pray you break down walls when you'd rather build them high. I pray you laugh without fear and let your imperfections become the starting point for your next intentional step.

Big steppers are ground takers. Ground takers become barrier breakers. Barrier breakers are freedom makers, and freedom makers are culture shapers and world changers. They're among the few who know how to do small things that truly become big things—with humble hands and fearless hearts.

Be among the few. Stop being passive and start living with passion. Don't wait for something good to happen—*be* the good that happens. Do hard things even when life is hard, right where you are, with what you have. Start small because small wins add up to big victories.

There's a hurting world out there, and your full yes—your willingness to show up right where you are in your corner of the universe—is what will change it. But saying yes to one thing means saying no to other things. Make your yes count. It does make a difference, and our yeses together add up.

Call that neighbor; talk to that coworker; take the first step toward starting that business. You don't need to see the whole path to live your purpose, and you don't need money, certifications, or all your plans ready to take a step. You just need to put your full yes on the table and claim that wildly glorious, hard, holy, and humble step right before you.

And when you fail, fail forward. Keep your eyes fixed ahead, not on what's behind you or who's to your left or right.

It's your turn now.

What's one small thing you can do today with a fearless heart? What's your next big step to unleashing the gift that lives in you and sharing it with the world right where you are? No more excuses. No more lies or labels. No more barriers. No more hiding behind doors. It's time to dance through doorways. I'm holding your hand. I'm rooting for you.

Because *you,* sister friend, are not an accident. You are not merely a work in progress. You are a woman of purpose, uniquely chosen to change today's world. Stop trying to be fancy or measure up. Just show up and be faithful where you are, with what you have. Don't let the pressure to prove get in the way. And watch what happens.

Ready, set, *own your everyday.*

Yes, girl, I hope you do big things
and go after your wildest dreams.
But guess what? To do the big,
cool things, you gotta start with
and show up for the small,
not-so-cool everyday things.
There is no way around that.

OWN YOUR EVERYDAY

Acknowledgments

To Matt, my love, for looking me in the eye when I almost quit and reminding me who I am, for listening to endless brainstorms and edits on long car rides, and for loving me enough to really listen and give honest, godly feedback. You helped shape not only these pages into what they've become but also the woman and wife I've become. You dared me to embrace the purpose I'm made for on the days I wanted to quit. I couldn't have done this without you.

To Mom, for your continued dedication as my number one fan. You were the wind beneath my fragile wings, and you taught me how to fly. Your faithfulness to God and commitment to our family have been the greatest examples of purpose in my life. Thank you for daring me to dream, pushing me to pray, and reminding me to rest. These pages have undeniable traces of your heart, and I am grateful.

To Dad, for teaching me to go after life with reckless abandon. Your dedication to excellence and your big heart for people change the world of those around you. You've not only kept me safe but also sent me out. When I left home at eighteen, I promised to honor your last name. That last name may not be printed on the cover of this book, but I hope you know it's influenced the words inside.

To Nick, for helping me have the kind of faith that walks on water. You're not just my brother; you're also my best friend. Because of you I've learned how to persevere and trust in God's faithfulness against all odds. You are a gift and an example. I love you.

To Grandma and Grandpa, for giving me a solid foundation and for setting an example of what hard work, service, and purpose look like in daily life. Your devotion, encouragement, and refreshing honesty challenge me to focus on the things that matter most. You've played a big part in shaping me into who I am today, and for that I'm forever grateful. Love and hugs to you both.

To Susan Tjaden and the WaterBrook team, for believing in me when I didn't believe in myself. You not only saw the potential, but you also saw this through. I'm endlessly grateful for your hard work and dedication to excellence. Thank you so much.

To my mentors, girlfriends, team, and family, for helping me through my insecurities, reminding me of my identity, and championing me every step of the way. The late-night texts, ongoing brainstorming sessions, purpose-filled prayers, and endless encouragement have made all the difference in the making of this book. I thank God for each one of you. You know who you are.

To my beloved launch team, for believing in this project and championing it so well. I truly couldn't have done this without you.

Notes

1. See Mark 8:36.
2. Dr. Jordan Peterson, "Biblical Series IX: The Call to Abraham," https://jordanbpeterson.com/transcripts /biblical-series-ix.
3. See James 5:16.
4. Brené Brown, *Rising Strong: How the Ability to Reset Transforms the Way We Live, Love, Parent, and Lead* (New York: Random House, 2015), 4.
5. See 2 Corinthians 10:5.
6. See Philippians 2:14–15.
7. *Merriam-Webster,* s.v. "perfectionism," www.merriam -webster.com/dictionary/perfectionism.
8. "Perfectionism," *Psychology Today,* www.psychology today.com/basics/perfectionism, emphasis added.
9. Dr. Wayne W. Dyer, Facebook, November 26, 2009, www.facebook.com/drwaynedyer/posts/i-am-a-human -being-not-a-human-doing-dont-equate-your-self-worth -with-how-well-y/185464583996.
10. Proverbs 4:23, NIV.
11. See Ecclesiastes 2:24.

12. Claire Gibson, "Making Room for the Stranger," *She Reads Truth* (blog), http://shereadstruth.com/2017/02 /07/making-room-for-the-stranger.

Join the Party!

If you liked *Own Your Everyday*, continue the conversation
and find even more resources at jordanleedooley.com.

To keep up with Jordan or to get involved
in her growing community, follow along here:

Podcast: jordanleedooley.com/podcast
Blog: jordanleedooley.com/blog
Instagram: @jordanleedooley
Facebook: @jordanleedooley
Twitter: @mrsjordandooley
Pinterest: jordanleedooley